A Call to
Reflection:
A Teacher's Guide to Catholic Identity for the 21st Century

Gini Shimabukuro, Ed.D.

DEPARTMENT OF ELEMENTARY SCHOOLS
NATIONAL CATHOLIC EDUCATIONAL ASSOCIATION
WASHINGTON, DC

ISBN #1-55833-205-7

BK
$8.00

"The more completely an educator
can give concrete witness
to the model of the ideal person
that is being presented to the students,
the more this ideal will be believed and imitated.
For it will then be seen as something
reasonable and worthy of being lived,
something concrete and realizable."

—Sacred Congregation for Catholic Education,
Lay Catholics in Schools: Witnesses to Faith, 1982, #32

Contents

Acknowledgments

Special appreciation is extended to two Catholic educators who typify the ideals described in this book: Sister Mary Peter Traviss, OP, director of the Institute for Catholic Educational Leadership at the University of San Francisco, and Father Edwin J. McDermott, SJ, faculty and former director of the institute, who both in their unique ways encouraged and promoted my exploration and study of the vital area of Catholic identity in the context of Catholic schooling.

Sincerest thanks to Dr. Marcy Fox, chair of the religious studies department at Carondelet High School, Concord, California, for her invaluable assistance in refining the manuscript for this book. Marcy is a "teacher of teachers," who exemplifies the ideal of the Catholic school scholar-practitioner.

Finally, but most importantly, thanks to my dear husband and sons, without whose love and patience I could never have embarked upon a project such as this.

List of Tables

Foreword

Jesus shared with you his teaching ministry. Only in close communion with him can you respond adequately. This is my hope, this is my prayer: that you will be totally open to Christ. That he will give you an ever greater love for your students and an ever stronger commitment to your vocation as Catholic educators. If you continue to be faithful to this ministry today, as you have been in the past, you will be doing much in shaping a peaceful, just and hope-filled world for the future. Yours is a great gift to the Church, a great gift to your nation.

—*Pope John Paul II, September 12, 1987, address to
Catholic educators, New Orleans, LA*

These words of Pope John Paul II draw attention to the fact that we Catholic educators perform a very important ministry in the Catholic Church. He also emphasizes that we teaching ministers must have a close relationship with Christ. The Catholic identity of our schools resides in a special way in ourselves. The more closely we teaching ministers mirror the life and teachings of Jesus, the more brightly the Catholic identity of our schools shines forth.

Key elements in our becoming more effective teaching ministers are our knowledge of what it means to cooperate with Christ in spreading his word and a time to reflect on our relationship with Christ. These are the two foundation stones on which *A Call to Reflection* are built.

Dr. Gini Shimabukuro has carefully studied all the Church documents on this topic and brought together in this book the most relevant passages. She has presented these around five themes:

Teacher as Community Builder
Teacher as Committed to Lifelong Spiritual Growth
Teacher as Committed to Professional Development
Teacher as Committed to Students' Spiritual Formation
Teacher as Committed to Students' Human Development

The presentation clearly indicates that our spiritual development is intimately connected with our apostolic work.

This is not a book that is to be read from cover to cover in one sitting. It is to be read thoughtfully and reflectively. Throughout the book are questions that we ministers should reflect upon, and space is provided for us to record a response. The book is a journal for spiritual growth.

This is a book that needs to be read many times over, because as we deepen our relationship with Christ, our reflections will take on new directions and insights.

The NCEA Department of Elementary Schools expresses its gratitude to Dr. Shimabukuro for developing this reflective manual for Catholic educators. Many people contributed to the production of this publication. Tara McCallum of the NCEA Department of Elementary Schools served as chief editor. Sister Ann Sciannella, also on the Department's staff, assisted with the retyping of the manuscript. Beatriz Ruiz of the NCEA Communications Department created the cover and laid out the pages. To these individuals and all others who assisted, the Department expresses its deep gratitude.

The NCEA Department of Elementary Schools presents this book to all its members with the hope that it will be a means of drawing all more closely to Christ.

Feast of St. John Baptist de La Salle, 1998
Patron of Teachers

Kieran Hartigan, RSM   *Robert J. Kealey, Ed.D.*
President   *Executive Director*

Department of Elementary Schools
National Catholic Educational Association

Introduction

Catholic Teacher Identity

Clarification of Catholic identity among Catholic school teachers is one of the greatest challenges facing Catholic schools today. It is an issue of critical importance, affecting the future of Catholic education globally. Confusion on behalf of its members divides a school and creates areas of "hidden" curricula that sabotage Gospel-driven educational goals. There is an urgency today to nurture our students into healthy, faith-filled, peacemaking adults who will not only function in, but also will provide stability and morality to, a technologically driven 21st-century society, which will only continue to be marked by innovation, change, and instability. Underlying the successful accomplishment of this critical goal must be unity among us, as Catholic educators, regarding the fundamentals of Catholic pedagogy.

The purpose of this book is to provide a reflective process through which you may consider your distinctness as an educator in a Catholic school. It will begin with a discussion of contemporary world and Catholic paradigms of thinking. These paradigms impact your role in unprecedented ways and suggest a framework for considering Catholic education in the 21st century. Catholic paradigms are rooted in major Church documents on education that were released during and since the Second Vatican Council of the mid-1960s. An analysis of these documents revealed five repetitive themes that form a "model" of the *ideal* Catholic school educator. They typify the teacher as being committed to:

- Community Building
- Lifelong Spiritual Growth
- Lifelong Professional Development
- Students' Spiritual Formation
- Students' Human Development

Throughout this book, each theme will be discussed in the context of the Church documents and then will be related to the realities of today's classrooms. Immediately preceding the discussion of each theme is a teacher self-inventory that you may tally and record on page 66 in order to self-assess your effectiveness in specific areas and to examine your perception of your overall effectiveness as a Catholic school educator. Following thematic discussions are "Questions for Reflection," which provide opportunities for you to deliberate on the real-life implications of the texts discussed. A section titled "To the Administrator" offers suggestions for implementing these materials with entire faculties, as well as additional activities.

Let us begin by reviewing the impact of the Second Vatican Council on the contemporary world of the Church and its schools.

New Paradigms: Catholic Identity and the Second Vatican Council

The Second Vatican Council convened in Rome in 1962. Adrian Hastings (1991), a professor of theology at the University of Leeds, characterized the phenomenal shift that was about to occur in the Church, recalling that once Pope John XXIII had called the Council, ". . . the consequences were inevitable: the foundations of many hundred years were going to be rocked upon every side" (p. 4). Hastings related that ". . . the world of the twentieth century again necessitated a quite extraordinarily different Church and theology from that appropriate in the past" (p. 7).

The Council fathers ushered in Pope John's call for *aggiornamento*, ecumenical understanding and cooperation with other Christians, with plans for its effective implementation, but, as Hastings (1991) related, ". . . people . . . saw it as, all in all, a daring and radical reform which had gone beyond anything they sought when the Council began" (p. 6). According to John McDade, SJ (1991), the Second Vatican Council proposed ". . . that the Church ought to be characterized by a profound engagement with the reality of the world's experience: no longer a Church set apart from the world within an institutional Christendom, but a Church that enters into profound solidarity with the experiences of human society, and takes humanity seriously in the unfolding of its history" (p. 422).

Table 1 describes the pre- and post-Vatican II Church, which was synchronizing with a changing world. Theologian Karl Rahner (1972) characterized society during this period as "the world of an immense future in process of being planned" (p. 6).

Table 1. Paradigm Shift in the Catholic Church (Pre-Vatican II to Post-Vatican II)

From:	To:
Hierarchical	Collaborative
Institutional	Community-based
Silent	Communicative
Dogmatic	Open to inquiry
Authoritarian	Participative
Static	Dynamic
Depersonalized	Individualized
Formative/Children	Developmental/Adults
Role-oriented	Person-oriented
Denominational	Ecumenical
Legalistic	Spirit-driven
Individual	Relational

The Second Vatican Council greatly impacted Catholic education. Twenty-three years after the Council published the *Declaration on Christian Education*, the Congregation for Catholic Education (1988) reiterated "an important advance in the way a Catholic school is thought of: the transition from the school as an institution to the school as a community" (#31). This was a significant shift in emphasis in the Catholic school from institutional observances and hierarchy to individual formation in the context of the community.

Today's Catholic School Teacher

Individual student formation in the context of a classroom community, a post-Vatican II concept, implies a great deal for today's Catholic school teacher. The challenges facing today's teacher are unmatched in American history. Confusion prevails regarding the role of the teacher in the context of the Catholic school, as well as in a changing society. In addition, societal pressures impinge upon the lives of our students like never before. Yet, the research consistently reports that in spite of a student's unfortunate home conditions, the educator can nevertheless make a significant impact on the lives of students. The *Catholic* educator can take this a step further by instilling in students the vital life dimensions of Christian faith and hope within a society marked by rising depression and suicide among its young, and concern for others in a society that cultivates narcissism through the media.

Never has it been more important for the teacher to be in touch with social realities (e.g., technological advances, cultural diversity, an endangered ecology, moral relativism, decline of the family) in order to assist students to develop the coping skills based upon a solid foundation of moral decision making. The effective teacher must be in touch with his or her audience of students on a daily basis, aware of the societal pressures that they are combatting, in order to create an authentic sense of community in the classroom. Remaining cognizant of social trends, therefore, is key to Catholic teacher effectiveness.

During and since Vatican II, a number of Church documents dealing with Catholic education have been published (see Table 2 below), serving as guideposts to Catholic educators in defining their distinguishing roles in the context of a new society. The following sections will provide a five-point model for considering Catholic school-teacher identity based upon the documents.

Table 2. Catholic Documents on Education, 1965-1990

Declaration on Christian Education	1965
To Teach as Jesus Did	1972
Teach Them	1976
The Catholic School	1977
Sharing the Light of Faith: National Catechetical Directory for Catholics of the United States	1979
Lay Catholics in Schools: Witnesses to Faith	1982
The Religious Dimension of Education in a Catholic School	1988
In Support of Catholic Elementary and Secondary Schools	1990

QUESTIONS FOR REFLECTION

1. *What is distinctive about my school?*

    _____

    _____

    _____

    _____

    _____

    _____

    _____

    _____

2. *How do I characterize the major differences between the Catholic approach to education and other approaches?*

    _____

    _____

    _____

    _____

    _____

    _____

    _____

    _____

    _____

3. *What are my students' social attitudes and practices? (For example, how much daily television do they watch? What are they watching? Do they have Internet access on home/school computers? If so, what are they accessing? What are their attitudes about religion, faith, family, relationships, love, sex, violence, peacemaking? Are they hopeful individuals, or are they dominated by hopelessness?)*

    _____

    _____

    _____

    _____

    _____

    _____

    _____

    _____

4. *Which Christian ideals do I reflect in my attitudes and practices with my students?*

    _____

    _____

    _____

    _____

_____
_____
_____

5. *Do I really believe that I can make a difference in the lives of my students? If so, in what ways? If not, why not?*

_____
_____
_____
_____
_____
_____
_____
_____

6. *Do I believe that the Catholic approach to education can substantially fortify a changing society? If so, in what ways?*

_____
_____
_____
_____
_____
_____
_____
_____
_____

Recommended Readings

Johnson, S. (1989). *Christian spiritual formation in the Church and classroom*. Nashville: Abingdon Press.

Kelly, F. D. (Ed.). (1991). *What makes a school Catholic?* Washington, DC: National Catholic Educational Association.

McDermott, E. J. (1996). *Distinctive qualities of the Catholic school*. Washington, DC: National Catholic Educational Association.

Moore, M. E. (1991). *Teaching from the heart: Theology and educational method*. Minneapolis: Fortress Press.

Mullin, M. (1991). *Educating for the 21st century*. Lanham, MD: Madison Books.

O'Keefe, J. (Ed.). (1996). *The contemporary Catholic school: Context, identity and diversity*. Great Britain: Biddles Ltd., Guildford and King's Lynn.

THEMES OVERVIEW:

The Ideal Catholic School Teacher

T he Catholic literature on education from 1965 to 1990 revealed five recurrent themes descriptive of the Catholic school teacher, depicting the teacher as a community builder who is additionally committed to his or her ongoing personal spiritual/religious formation and professional development and to the spiritual/religious formation and human development of his or her students (see Appendixes A and B). This is a simultaneous process in which the teacher's formation, both spiritually and professionally, continually impacts his or her efforts to promote student formation. One aspect without the other, that is, total focus on student formation without ongoing teacher formation, potentially cripples this wholistic approach to education.

In reference to the wholistic aspect of Catholic education, Bowman (1990) elaborated on this idea, referring to Catholic education as "organismic":

> If we begin to speak of any one [part of the whole], we find ourselves drawn to include the others. And all such speaking can occur without any necessity to place [other parts of the whole] . . . in some sort of order or hierarchy. We do not list the [parts] . . . in some preferred arrangement; we do not attempt to fit them into a diagram. They meld into one another in a foundational complex. (p. 40)

Although we will examine the parts of this model individually, it must not be forgotten that each part fits into an organic, interrelated foundation, upon which the Catholic approach to education is based. Symbolic of Vatican II thinking, which cautioned against compartmentalized ideas with static interpretations, this model functions through connectivity and fluidity. In practical terms, this means that the teacher, in the most profound sense, is a "reflective practitioner" (Schön, 1983) who continuously strives to develop his or her spiritual, religious, and professional self while promoting the spiritual, religious, and human development of the students. Moreover, true formation of the teacher, as well as of the students, cannot occur in isolation. It must take place in the context of a community, which brings forth the significant theme of the teacher as a community builder.

THEME ONE:
Teacher as Community Builder

TEACHER SELF-INVENTORY

Community Building

Directions: For a self-evaluation of your skills in building community among your students, complete the following items. For each item enter the number that most closely depicts the frequency of your experience. Enter your scores on page 66 to create a personal profile.

	Consistently 4	Often 3	Seldom 2	Never 1
As a Catholic school educator:				
1. Do I affirm the dignity of each student whom I teach?	_____	_____	_____	_____
2. Do I appreciate the diversity (cultures, personal talents, religions, etc.) of my students and concretely instill this appreciation in them?	_____	_____	_____	_____
3. Do I consciously employ skills and strategies with my students to create a sense of community among them?	_____	_____	_____	_____
4. Do I strive to develop healthy, caring relationships with my students?	_____	_____	_____	_____
5. Do I encourage my students to become peacemakers, locally as well as globally?	_____	_____	_____	_____
6. Do I collaborate with fellow teachers at every opportunity, e.g., through prayer and worship, team teaching, school events?	_____	_____	_____	_____
7. Do I acknowledge that parents are the primary educators of their children and create partnerships with my students' parents?	_____	_____	_____	_____
8. Do I support the "shared vision," the written philosophy, of my school in tangible ways?	_____	_____	_____	_____
9. Do I encourage my students to provide service to others within the school?	_____	_____	_____	_____
10. Do I create opportunities for my students to become involved in service projects to the larger community outside the school?	_____	_____	_____	_____

Total: _____ = _____ + _____ + _____ + _____

● *Areas in which I am most proud as a community builder with my students:*

_____

_____

_____

_____

_____

_____

_____

_____

_____

_____

● *Areas in which I could improve community among my students:*

_____

_____

_____

_____

_____

_____

_____

_____

_____

_____

The Message of the Church Documents

In order to understand the role of the teacher as a community builder in the context of Catholic education, it is necessary first to explore the meaning of Christian *community*, a foundational concept. The document *To Teach as Jesus Did* forcefully defined Christian community in the following manner:

> As God's plan unfolds in the life of an individual Christian, he grows in awareness that, as a child of God, he does not live in isolation from others. From the moment of Baptism he becomes a member of a new and larger family, the Christian community. Reborn in Baptism, he is joined to others in common faith, hope, and love. This community is based not on force or accident of geographic location or even on deeper ties of ethnic origin, but on the life of the Spirit which unites its members in a unique fellowship so intimate that Paul likens it to a body of which each individual is a part and Jesus Himself is the Head. In this community one person's problem is everyone's problem and one person's victory is everyone's victory. Never before and never since the coming of Jesus Christ has anyone proposed such a community. (National Conference of Catholic Bishops, 1972, #22)

Thus, the Catholic educational community may be identified by members who share faith, hope, and love.

According to the authors of the document *Sharing the Light of Faith: National Catechetical Directory for Catholics of the United States*, the breakdown of the family, along with the deterioration of community identity in contemporary American society, demands that educators "no longer take for granted a sense of community . . . [but] instead work to develop and sustain it" (National Conference of Catholic Bishops, 1979, #21). M. Scott Peck (1987), in his book *The Different Drum*, demonstrated the psychological sophistication and the potential study involved in an authentic understanding of the concept of community:

> Community is integrative. It includes people of different sexes, ages, religions, cultures, viewpoints, life styles, and stages of development by integrating them into a whole that is greater—better—than the sum of its parts. Integration is not a melting process; it does not result in a bland average. Rather, it has been compared to the creation of a salad in which the identity of the individual ingredients is preserved yet simultaneously transcended. Community does not solve the problem of pluralism by obliterating diversity. Instead it seeks out diversity, welcomes other points of view, embraces opposites, desires to see the other side of every issue. It is "wholistic." It integrates us human beings into a functioning mystical body. (p. 234)

In *To Teach as Jesus Did*, the idea of individual formation within the context of community was identified as forming "persons-in-community" (National Conference of Catholic Bishops, 1972, #13). Thus, it is through the community that the individual is able to acquire an identity, a sense of his or her personhood. Reciprocally, each individual directly affects the functioning of the community to which he or she belongs.

Formation that occurs within the context of a community was elaborated on in *The Religious Dimension of Education in a Catholic School*. The authors of this document stated, "In pedagogical circles, today as in the past, great stress is put on the climate of a school: the sum total of the different components at work in the school which interact with one another in such a way as to create favorable conditions for a formation process" (Congregation for Catholic Education, 1988, #24). These "different components," which form an organic vision of the climate of the school, consist in "persons, space, time, relationships, teaching, study, and various other activities" (#24), the authors explained. Combined, they create a synergy that distinguishes the Catholic school community from any other educational institution. According to the document authors, "From the first moment that a student sets foot in a Catholic school, he or she ought to have the impression of entering a new environment, one illumined by the light of faith, and having its own unique characteristics" (#25). The authors of this document placed primary responsibility for the creation of this unique Christian climate in the school with the teachers, acknowledging, however, that "the students are not spectators . . . [but] help to determine the quality of this climate" (#103). Additional creators of school climate include administrative and auxiliary staff, parents, directors, and all others associated with the school community.

The Religious Dimension of Education in a Catholic School created the metaphor of a "school-home" (Congregation for Catholic Education, 1988, #27) for the Catholic school, an extension of the home, demonstrating the extent to which teachers are asked to develop a unique climate. The authors of this Church document elaborated on the concept of the school-home as promoting a climate that is "humanly and spiritually rich" (#28) and that "reproduces, as far as possible, the warm and intimate atmosphere of family life" (#40) and exudes a "common spirit of trust and spontaneity" (#40). The document authors explained:

> "School" is often identified with "teaching"; actually, classes and lessons are only a small part of school life. Along with the lessons that a teacher gives, there is the active participation of the students individually or as a group: study, research, exercises, para-curricular activities, examinations, relationships with teachers and with one another, group activities, class meetings, school assemblies. (#47)

Jean Roland Martin (1992) developed this metaphor of the school as a school-home into a book carrying that precise title. She emphatically stated, "Our challenge is to turn the schoolhouse into the Schoolhome: a moral equivalent of home for our young that will be . . . responsive to the needs and conditions of children and their parents at the end of the twentieth century" (p. 33).

As one who integrates self and students into what Peck (1987) called "the functioning mystical body" of the Catholic school community, the teacher, throughout the Church documents on education cited, is encouraged to strive to (a) participate in the shared vision, the written philosophy, of the school; (b) affirm the dignity of each student; (c) appreciate student diversity; (d) teach to issues of peace and justice; (e) develop caring relationships with students; (f) collaborate with colleagues and parents; and (g) integrate service into the curriculum. Let us consider each of these community-related themes in light of the Church documentation on education.

Participating in the Shared Vision of the School. The *Declaration on Christian Education* identified the Catholic school community as having "an atmosphere animated by a spirit of liberty and charity based on the Gospel" (Second Vatican Council, 1965/1988, #8). *Sharing the Light of Faith: National Catechetical Directory for Catholics of the United States* urged educators to actively participate in this special atmosphere by proactively sharing in the Christian vision of the school community. Its authors recommended that every aspect of the school community be involved in a carefully planned process to develop a philosophy, goals and objectives, and other important components of the school. Moreover, *The Religious Dimension of Education in a Catholic School* called for unity among teachers in order for the religious dimension of the school to be realized:

> . . . what really matters is not the terminology but the reality, and this reality will be assured only if all the teachers unite their educational efforts in the pursuit of a common goal. Sporadic, partial, or uncoordinated efforts, or a situation in which there is a conflict of opinion among the teachers, will interfere with rather than assist in the students' personal development. (Congregation for Catholic Education, 1988, #99)

The summons to a shared Christian vision enforces the identity and future of the Catholic school. In *The Catholic School*, the Sacred Congregation for Catholic Education (1977) declared that "Catholic teachers who freely accept posts in [Catholic] schools, which have a distinctive character, are obliged to respect that character and give their active support to it" (#80). Hence, the congregation continued, "if all who are responsible for the Catholic school would never lose sight of their mission and the apostolic value of their teaching, the school would enjoy better conditions in which to function in the present and would faithfully hand on its mission to future generations" (#87).

Affirming the Dignity of Each Student and ***Appreciating Student Diversity.*** Intrinsic to the Gospel-based environment of the school is the realization and implementation of individual dignity, in which "the pupil experiences his dignity as a person before he knows its definition" (Sacred Congregation for Catholic Education, 1977, #55). Throughout the documents on Catholic education, the value for the individual is emphatically proclaimed. *Lay Catholics in Schools: Witnesses to Faith* further stated:

> It must never be forgotten that, in the crises "which have their greatest effect on the younger generations," the most important element in the educational endeavor is "always the individual person: the person, and the moral dignity of that person which is the result of his or her principles, and the conformity of actions with those principles." (Sacred Congregation for Catholic Education, 1982, #32)

The Religious Dimension of Education in a Catholic School encapsulated the Christian vision of human dignity:

> The religious dimension makes a true understanding of the human person possible. A human being has a dignity and a greatness exceeding that of all other creatures: a work of God that has been elevated to the supernatural order of a child of God, and therefore having both a divine origin and an eternal destiny which transcend this physical universe. Religion teachers will find the way already prepared for an organic presentation of Christian anthropology. (Congregation for Catholic Education, 1988, #56)

Valuing the individual implies appreciating student diversity. Teachers are called to adapt the educational process "in a way that respects the particular circumstances of individual students and their families" (Congregation for Catholic Education, 1988, #101). With the non-Catholic student, this translates into a demonstration of respect with an openness to dialogue in the context of Christian love.

Teaching to Peace and Justice. Teachers are urged to cultivate a global consciousness for a more just society and to apply justice principles to the immediate community of the Catholic school. These involve providing the appropriate support of social action and assisting in finding solutions to "a host of complex problems such as war, poverty, racism, and environmental pollution which undermines community within and among nations" (National Conference of Catholic Bishops, 1979, #210). *Lay Catholics in Schools: Witnesses to Faith* summarized the responsibility of the Catholic educator in this regard:

> The vocation of every Catholic educator includes the work of ongoing social development: to form men and women who will be ready to take their place in society, preparing them in such a way that they will make the kind of social commitment which will enable them to work for the improvement of social structures, making these structures more conformed to the principles of the Gospel. (Sacred Congregation for Catholic Education, 1982, #19)

Developing Caring Relationships with Students. The concept of the school-home, mentioned in *The Religious Dimension of Education in a Catholic School*, is intimately connected to the teacher as one who builds caring relationships with students. This document, more than any other, developed this theme. Simply talking with students and allowing them to talk is suggested as an excellent method for establishing rapport with students. After "a warm and trusting atmosphere has been established, various questions will come up naturally. . . . These questions are serious ones for young people, and they make a calm study of the Christian faith very difficult" (Congregation for Catholic Education, 1988, #72). The authors of this document advised teachers to respond with patience and humility and to "avoid the type of peremptory statements that can be so easily contradicted" (#72). Parker Palmer (1985), in *To Know as We Are Known: A Spirituality of Education*, illuminated the notion of humility, a vital virtue to be possessed by the teacher engaged in establishing rapport with students:

> Humility is the virtue that allows us to pay attention to "the other"—be it student or subject—whose integrity and voice are so central to knowing and teaching in truth. Its opposite is the sin of pride, once defined by G. K. Chesterton as "seeing oneself out of proportion to the universe." In the words of Karl Deutsch, humility is "an attitude towards facts and messages outside oneself, . . . openness to experience as well as to criticism . . . a sensitivity and responsiveness to the needs and desires of others." . . . Humility not only creates a space in which the other can speak; it also allows us to enter into obedience to the other, . . . trying

to hear the reality behind . . . [the] students' plea, wondering how to respond faithfully to it. (pp. 108-109)

The Catholic School beautifully described the relational component of the Catholic environment when it stated: "It [the Catholic school] wants to share their [young people's] anxieties and their hopes as it, indeed, shares their present and future lot in this world" (Sacred Congregation for Catholic Education, 1977, #57). Catholic educators were called to be psychologically present to their students. *Lay Catholics in Schools: Witnesses to Faith* advised teachers that they must adhere to pedagogical theory that is Christian-based, "which gives special emphasis to direct and personal contact with the students" (Sacred Congregation for Catholic Education, 1982, #21). Openness and readiness for dialogue with students, with an awareness that the enrichment is mutual, is key to building student relationships. Not simply a methodology for their formation, direct and personal contact with students, according to this document, constitutes "the means by which teachers learn what they need to know about the students in order to guide them adequately" (#33). The document stated further:

> . . . rapport with the students ought to be a prudent combination of familiarity and distance; and this must be adapted to the need of each individual student. Familiarity will make a personal relationship easier, but a certain distance is also needed: students need to learn how to express their own personality without being pre-conditioned; they need to be freed from inhibitions in the responsible exercise of their freedom. (#33)

Advocating that teachers resolutely foster student relationships, *Lay Catholics in Schools* authors counseled: "The difference in generation is deeper, and the time between generations is shorter, today more than ever before; direct contact [between teacher and student], then, is more necessary than ever" (Sacred Congregation for Catholic Education, 1982, #33). Henri Nouwen (1971), in *Creative Ministry*, emphasized the importance of this dimension of the Catholic school when he wrote, "Perhaps we have paid too much attention to the content of teaching without realizing that the teaching relationship is the most important factor in the ministry of teaching" (p. 5).

Collaborating with Colleagues and Parents. *Collaboration*, a word which immediately characterizes new-paradigm thinking, received specific focus in *Lay Catholics in Schools: Witnesses to Faith*. In regard to teachers collaborating with colleagues, this document stated that "close relationship should be established with one's colleagues; they should work together as a team" (Sacred Congregation for Catholic Education, 1982, #34); "the Church depends on lay collaboration" (#58); and "before all else, lay people should find in a Catholic school an atmosphere of sincere respect and cordiality; it should be a place in which authentic human relationships can be formed among all of the educators" (#77).

According to *The Religious Dimension of Education in a Catholic School*, collaboration between teachers and parents, a "partnership based on faith" (Congregation for Catholic Education, 1988, #42), insists upon an integration of the school with the home, which is essential to the realization of the potential development of children. Parents, in this document, are acknowledged as the "first and primary educators of children" (#43), with teachers as partners in the educational endeavor. This implies that parents participate with the school and that teachers assist the education of parents. Meetings and programs to raise the consciousness of parents in this regard are recommended. Also acknowledging the primacy of the family, *Lay Catholics in Schools: Witnesses to Faith* contained a directive to teachers:

The family is "the first and fundamental school of social living" therefore, there is a special duty to accept willingly and even to encourage opportunities for contact with the parents of students. These contacts are very necessary, because the educational task of the family and that of the school complement one another in many concrete areas; and they will facilitate the "serious duty" that parents have "to commit themselves totally to a cordial and active relationship with the teachers and the school authorities." Finally, such contacts will offer to many families the assistance they need in order to educate their own children properly, and thus fulfill the "irreplaceable and inalienable" function that is theirs. (Sacred Congregation for Catholic Education, 1982, #34)

Integrating Service into the Curriculum. Finally, teacher collaboration with the human community outside the school includes the development of students' social awareness within their communities through service opportunities; close teacher relationships with groups within the Catholic and the secular educational communities at large; teacher awareness of the sociocultural, economic, and political aspects of the local community of the school; national and international community awareness; and outreach to other Catholic schools as well as to Christian and public schools. As written in *The Religious Dimension of Education in a Catholic School*, "Christian education sees all of humanity as one large family, divided perhaps by historical and political events, but always one in God who is Father of all" (Congregation for Catholic Education, 1988, #45).

The role of the Catholic school educator as a community builder is an all-encompassing ministerial call. Catholic school teachers, at their authentic best, realize that community building constitutes the very essence of their role in the Catholic school.

Implementing the Message

In his thoughtful book *The Different Drum: Community Making and Peace*, M. Scott Peck (1987) identified *community* as

a group of individuals who have learned how to communicate honestly with each other, whose relationships go deeper than their masks of composure, and who have developed some significant commitment to "rejoice together, mourn together," and to "delight in each other, mak[ing] others' conditions [their] own." (p. 59)

His definition complements that offered in the 1972 Church document *To Teach as Jesus Did*, which related that a Christian community is one in which "one person's problem is everyone's problem and one person's victory is everyone's victory" (National Conference of Catholic Bishops, #22). The contemporary Catholic school is teeming with diversity among the student and parent populations. The teacher is truly challenged to work toward the ideal of *authentic* Christian community.

M. Scott Peck (1987), in his book, continued to point out the relationship between *community* and *communication*, both derived from the Latin root word meaning "to make common." *Unity*, which exists in the word *community*, is achieved by recognizing and promoting commonalities. These are discovered through communication. Thus, efforts toward community building must necessarily involve effective communication, which implies that the Catholic school teacher must be an *effective communicator*. Such teachers are equipped with a variety of interpersonal and communication skills, a positive self-concept, and an openness to vulnerability, which is the essence of authentic community. They regularly monitor and seek to develop their psychological, spiritual, and moral states of being as well as their patience and humility, the virtues that permit vulnerability in relationships with colleagues, students, and their families. The Church documents on education clearly summon Catholic school teachers to this sophisticated level of human interaction, which they are expected to re-create with their students in their classrooms. As community builders, these teachers are called to create safe, growth-conducive, potentially transformative, learning environments, in which students are encouraged to learn wholistically, in which students will risk the expression of their feelings as well as their "higher-order" thinking. When this is accomplished, the classroom simulates a family atmosphere, in which each student experiences a sense of belonging. Brain-based research on human learning has clearly established the correlation between optimal student performance and such an environment.

Teachers can greatly improve their community-building skills through inservice opportunities that focus on student self-esteem, moral development, multiculturalism, and conflict management. Taking the Myers-Briggs Personality Inventory offers an opportunity for teacher self-knowledge as well as an appreciation for the differing styles of colleagues and students.

QUESTIONS FOR REFLECTION

1. *If I knew that one of my students was destined to become an international figure who would impact the world, what kind of learning environment would I create for this student?*

_____

_____

_____

_____

_____

_____

_____

_____

_____

2. *On the basis of my response to the previous question, how would I formulate my vision for Catholic education?*

_____

_____

_____

_____

_____

_____

_____

_____

3. *How does my vision for Catholic education conform to, or differ from, my school's stated philosophy?*

_____

_____

_____

_____

_____

_____
_____
_____

4. *In what ways do I affirm the dignity of each student in my classroom?*

_____
_____
_____
_____
_____
_____
_____
_____

5. *In what ways do I affirm the dignity of my colleagues?*

_____
_____
_____
_____
_____
_____
_____
_____

6. *Specifically, how do I teach to peace and social justice issues?*

_____
_____
_____
_____
_____
_____
_____
_____

7. *How would I describe the rapport that I establish with my students?*

_____
_____
_____
_____
_____
_____

8. *What can I do to improve my relationships with my students?*

9. *In what ways do I collaborate with my colleagues?*

10. *What can be done to improve collaboration among teachers in my school?*

11. *In what ways do I establish partnerships with the parents of my students?*

12. *How do I assist in the education of the parents of my students?*

_____

_____

_____

_____

_____

_____

_____

_____

13. *What service opportunities for students are built into my curriculum?*

_____

_____

_____

_____

_____

_____

_____

_____

Teacher Resources

Bolton, R. (1979). *People skills: How to assert yourself, listen to others, and resolve conflicts.* New York: Simon & Schuster.

Borba, M. (1989). *Esteem builders* (Elementary level). Rolling Hills Estates, CA: Jalmar Press.

Borba, M. (1993). *Staff esteem builders.* Rolling Hills Estates, CA: Jalmar Press.

Caine, R. N., & Geoffrey, C. (1991). *Making connections: Teaching and the human brain.* Alexandria, VA: Association for Supervision and Curriculum Development.

Cowan, D., Palomares, S., & Schilling, D. (1993). *Teaching the skills of conflict resolution.* Spring Valley, CA: Innerchoice.

Faber, A., & Mazlish, E. (1980). *How to talk so kids will listen and listen so kids will talk.* New York: Avon Books.

Faber, A., & Mazlish, E. (1995). *How to talk so kids can learn at home and in school.* New York: Simon & Schuster.

Glasser, W. (1992). *The quality school: Managing students without coercion.* New York: HarperCollins.

Goleman, D. (1995). *Emotional intelligence.* New York: Bantam Books.

LaMeres, C. (1990). *The winner's circle: Yes, I can!* (Secondary level). Newport Beach, CA: LaMeres Lifestyles Unlimited.

Loomans, D., & Kolberg, K. (1993). *The laughing classroom: Everyone's guide to teaching with humor and play.* Tiburon, CA: H. J. Kramer.

McKay, M., Davis, M., & Fanning, P. (1983). *Messages: The communication skills book.* Oakland: New Harbinger Publications.

Nelsen, J., Lott, L., & Glenn, H. S. (1993). *Positive discipline in the classroom.* Rocklin, CA: Prima.

Reasoner, R. (1982). *Building self-esteem: A comprehensive program for schools.* Palo Alto, CA: Consulting Psychologists Press.

Sergiovanni, T. (1994). *Building community in schools.* San Francisco: Jossey-Bass.

Whitehead, E., & Whitehead, J. (1993). *Community of faith: Crafting Christian communities today.* Mystic, CT: Twenty-Third Publications.

THEME TWO:

Teacher as Committed to Lifelong Spiritual Growth

TEACHER SELF-INVENTORY

Lifelong Spiritual Growth

Directions: For a self-evaluation of your commitment to lifelong spiritual growth, complete the following items. For each item enter the number that most closely depicts the frequency of your experience. Enter your scores on page 66 to create a personal profile.

	Consistently 4	Often 3	Seldom 2	Never 1
As a Catholic school educator:				
1. Do I strive to deepen my understanding of the Catholic faith?	_____	_____	_____	_____
2. Do I view my teaching role as that of ministry?	_____	_____	_____	_____
3. Do I model reverence for the holy to my students?	_____	_____	_____	_____
4. Do I become involved in activities that nurture my continuing spiritual formation?	_____	_____	_____	_____
5. Do I consciously integrate Christian values into my curriculum and instruction?	_____	_____	_____	_____
6. Do I remain updated in Catholic doctrine/theology?	_____	_____	_____	_____
7. Do I model psychological well-being to my students and colleagues?	_____	_____	_____	_____
8. Do I reflect upon my effectiveness as a teacher in a Catholic school culture?	_____	_____	_____	_____
9. Do I engage with students individually and project a person-centered approach to my teaching?	_____	_____	_____	_____
10. Do I permeate the Christian spirit in my dealings with others (school personnel, parents, etc.) outside of my classroom?	_____	_____	_____	_____

Total: _____ = _____ + _____ + _____ + _____

● *Areas in which I am most proud of my commitment to my spiritual growth*:

_____
_____
_____
_____
_____
_____
_____
_____
_____
_____

● *Areas in which I could improve my commitment to my spiritual growth*:

_____
_____
_____
_____
_____
_____
_____
_____
_____
_____

The Message of the Church Documents

The Catholic dimension of the school finds its roots in each teacher's commitment to spiritual growth. Rather than view themselves strictly as a professional, Catholic school educators include in their identity the function of *minister*, of one who possesses a *vocation* to Catholic education. As stated in the *Declaration on Christian Education*, "This vocation requires special qualities of mind and heart" (Second Vatican Council, 1965/1988, #5). Since 1965, Church documents on education have delineated the precise nature of these mind-and-heart qualities. Let us examine a brief chronological description of these teacher characteristics as presented in the Church documents.

In the document *Teach Them*, specific emphasis was given to the *personhood* of the teacher: "Teachers' life style and character [are] as important as their professional credentials" (National Conference of Catholic Bishops, 1976, p. 7). This emphasis represented a shift from old-paradigm thinking, which focused upon conformity to an established, predetermined *role* of teacher that was static and compartmentalized rather than dynamic and relational. This new model, according to the document, called for teachers who "teach by what they are" (p. 3).

In 1977, *The Catholic School* continued to emphasize the person of the teacher, referring to the Catholic school professional as being engaged in an "authentic apostolate" (Sacred Congregation for Catholic Education, #63). The authenticity of the apostolate was characterized by engagement with students that is individualized, person centered, and relational:

Only one who has this conviction and accepts Christ's message, who has a love for and understands today's young people, who appreciates what people's real problems and difficulties are, will be led to contribute with courage and even audacity to the progress of this apostolate in building up a Catholic school, which puts its theory into practice, which renews itself according to its ideals and to present needs. (#83)

Intrinsic to the authentic apostolate of the Catholic school teacher is the daily witness of the teacher to his or her students through the modeling of Christian values. This document went so far as to state that achievement of the objectives of the Catholic school depends "not so much on subject matter or methodology as on the people who work there" (#43); that teachers must "reveal the Christian message not only by word but also by every gesture of their behaviour" (#43); and that "this is what makes the difference between a school whose education is permeated by the Christian spirit and one in which religion is only regarded as an academic subject like any other" (#43).

Lay Catholics in Schools: Witnesses to Faith further refined the concept of the vocation of the teacher: "The teacher under discussion here is not simply a professional person who systematically transmits a body of knowledge in the context of a school; 'teacher' is to be understood as 'educator'—one who helps to form human persons" (Sacred Congregation for Catholic Education, 1982, #16). In more detail, this document explained:

> . . . The lay Catholic educator is a person who exercises a specific mission within the Church by living, in faith, a secular vocation in the communitarian structure of the school: with the best possible professional qualifications, with an apostolic intention inspired by faith, for the integral formation of the human person, in a communication of culture, in an exercise of that pedagogy which will give emphasis to direct and personal contact with students, giving spiritual inspiration to the educational community of which he or she is a member, as well as to all the different persons related to the educational community. (#24)

The formation of students, particularly through the modeling of Christian values, is integral to the vocation of the Catholic school teacher. *Lay Catholics in Schools: Witnesses to Faith* stressed that the interior synthesis of the student "is, of course, a synthesis which should already exist in the teacher" (Sacred Congregation for Catholic Education, 1982, #29). Obviously, student formation is contingent upon teacher formation. The spiritual and religious formation of the teacher consist in personal sanctification and apostolic mission. According to this document, " 'Formation for apostolic mission means a certain human and well-rounded formation, adapted to the natural abilities and circumstances of each person' and requires 'in addition to spiritual formation, . . . solid doctrinal instruction . . . in theology, ethics and philosophy'" (#65). Furthermore, the teacher, the document authors point out, should receive "adequate formation in the social teachings of the Church, which are 'an integral part of the Christian concept of life,' and help to keep intensely alive the kind of social sensitivity that is needed" (#65). The consequence of teacher formation is immeasurable. The document warned, "Without it, the school will wander further and further away from its objectives" (#79).

Complementing the necessity for the spiritual and religious formation of teachers and the risks inherent in the neglect of this vital area, *The Religious Dimension of Education in a Catholic School* reinforced the vocation of the Catholic school teacher to involve "the celebration of Christian values in Word and Sacrament, in individual behavior, in friendly and harmonious interpersonal relationships, and in ready availability" (Congregation for Catholic Education, 1988, #26). Therein lies the religious dimension of the school. Without these components, "there is little left which can make the school Catholic" (#97).

Lay Catholics in Schools: Witnesses to Faith advised that the spiritual and religious dimensions of the Catholic school teacher "must be broadened and be kept up to date, on the same level as, and in harmony with, human formation as a whole" (Sacred Congregation for Catholic Education, 1982, #62). The document pointed out that a combination of spiritual formation with human formation constitutes "an appropriate professional competence" (#62) for the Catholic school teacher, which "does not come to an end with the completion of basic education" (#65). Finally, the assessment of the Catholic school teacher must embrace the religious dimension. *The Catholic School* and *Lay Catholics in Schools: Witnesses to Faith* recommended that the teacher engage in self-evaluation on the authenticity of his or her vocation to Catholic education. Although not elaborated upon at length, this theme cannot be overemphasized, as it is intimately linked to the pastoral formation process underlying the preparation of the Catholic school teacher.

Implementing the Message

As evidenced in the Church documents on education, the classic indicator of a Catholic school is a faculty who view themselves not only as professional educators but also as ministers of the faith. Prior to Vatican II, this self-identification was limited to those with a vocation to religious life. Today, when the majority of Catholic school teachers are laypersons, spiritual formation should be an ongoing priority of staff development.

It is vitally important that Catholic educators reflect on their commonalities of belief, exploring the Catholic faith dimension that distinctively defines each person's spirituality. Providing opportunities for written reflections and for voluntary sharing with one another, making prayer a priority among teachers, studying Catholic theology as a routine faculty inservice, celebrating liturgies together, engaging in retreats periodically—all attempt to build this critical dimension. It is this faith aspect that is most crucial to the Catholic identity of our schools. As declared in the document *Teach Them*, teachers "teach by what they are" (National Conference of Catholic Bishops, 1976, p. 3). They must be given opportunities to become spiritually and religiously *informed, formed,* and *transformed,* so they may sincerely model this vital dimension to students. Without this dimension, Catholic schools become reduced to secular schools. They may excel in community building, professionalism, and the wholistic development of students; however, devoid of the Catholic dimension as a lived reality in the school, they no longer reflect the Catholic identity of the school.

Reflective Activity

The following activity (source unknown) is designed to stimulate reflection of your spiritual journey. Simply, fill in the blanks as indicated, or create your own letter by developing one or two of the sentence starters.

A LETTER TO MYSELF ABOUT MY SPIRITUAL JOURNEY

Dear _____,

The earliest memory I have of coming to a sense of God is _____

_____

_____,

and when I remember that now, I _____

_____

_____

_____.

Other times were _____

_____

_____

_____

_____.

    The person(s) with whom I associate my spiritual growth is (are) _____

_____

_____

because _____

_____

_____

_____.

Other strong influences in my early spiritual life were _____

_____

_____

because _____

_____

_____

_____.

Currently, I am drawn in my journey by _____

_____

_____.

I feel that I am _____

_____

_____

_____.

    What I most want from life is _____

_____

_____

and _____

_____

_____
_____
_____.

People who are assisting me are _____
_____
_____
_____
_____.

People whom I am assisting are _____
_____
_____
_____
_____.

(Continue your letter with any additional reflections that pertain to your spiritual journey.)

QUESTIONS FOR REFLECTION

1. *How would I describe my vocation to Catholic education?*

_____
_____
_____
_____
_____
_____
_____
_____

2. *In what ways do I contribute to the Catholicity of my school?*

_____
_____
_____
_____
_____
_____
_____
_____

3. *Catholic school teachers are called to "teach by what they are." What special gifts do I bring to my students?*

_____

_____

_____

_____

_____

_____

_____

_____

_____

4. *What constitutes my prayer life?*

_____

_____

_____

_____

_____

_____

_____

_____

_____

5. *In what ways do I attempt to spiritually inspire my students?*

_____

_____

_____

_____

_____

_____

_____

_____

6. *To what extent do I share commonalities of the Catholic faith with my colleagues?*

_____

_____

_____

_____

_____

_____

_____

_____

Teacher Resources

Bednar, R. L., & Peterson, S. R. (1990). *Spirituality and self-esteem.* Salt Lake City: Deseret.

Brueggemann, W., Groome, T., & Parks, S. (1986). *Act justly, love tenderly, walk humbly.* New York: Paulist Press.

Buckley, F., & Sharp, D. (1986). *Deepening Christian life.* San Francisco: Harper & Row.

Eagan, J. F. (1995). *Restoration and renewal: The Church in the third millennium.* Kansas City, MO: Sheed & Ward.

Grant, W. H., Thompson, M., & Clarke, T. E. (1983). *From image to likeness: A Jungian path in the gospel journey.* New York: Paulist Press.

Groome, T. (1980). *Christian religious education: Sharing our story and vision.* San Francisco: Harper & Row.

Groome, T. (1991). *Sharing faith.* San Francisco: HarperCollins.

Harbaugh, G. L. (1990). *God's gifted people: Discovering your personality as a gift.* Minneapolis: Augsburg Fortress.

Harris, M. (1989). *Dance of the spirit: The seven steps of women's spirituality.* New York: Bantam Books.

Jacobs, R. M. (1996). *The vocation of the Catholic educator.* Washington, DC: National Catholic Educational Association.

Moore, T. (1992). *Care of the soul: A guide for cultivating depth and sacredness in everyday life.* New York: HarperCollins.

Richardson, P. T. (1996). *Four spiritualities.* Palo Alto, CA: Davies-Black.

Schmidt, J. (1989). *Praying our experiences.* Winona, MN: St. Mary's Press.

THEME THREE:

Teacher as Committed to Lifelong Professional Development

TEACHER SELF-INVENTORY

Lifelong Professional Development

Directions: For a self-evaluation of your commitment to lifelong professional development, complete the following items. For each item enter the number that most closely depicts the frequency of your experience. Enter your scores on page 66 to create a personal profile.

	Consistently 4	Often 3	Seldom 2	Never 1
As a Catholic school educator:				
1. Do I strive to remain updated in teaching methods that allow me to be a more effective teacher with my students?	____	____	____	____
2. Am I a *facilitator* of student learning?	____	____	____	____
3. Do I allow my students to participate in instructional decision making?	____	____	____	____
4. Am I a "reflective practitioner"?	____	____	____	____
5. Do I employ a variety of instructional methods with my students in order to teach to the *whole child* as well as to include a diversity of student learners?	____	____	____	____
6. Do I maintain an awareness of the realities of American society, and am I alert to how these realities affect the lives of my students?	____	____	____	____
7. Do I remain abreast of advances in technology?	____	____	____	____
8. Do I view myself as a lifelong learner?	____	____	____	____
9. Do I incorporate the use of technology in my teaching and in student learning?	____	____	____	____
10. Do I take advantage of opportunities for professional development (e.g., conferences, workshops)?	____	____	____	____

Total: _____ = ____ + ____ + ____ + ____

● *Areas in which I am most proud of my commitment to my professional growth*:

_____

_____

_____

_____

_____

_____

_____

_____

_____

● *Areas in which I could improve my commitment to my professional growth*:

_____

_____

_____

_____

_____

_____

_____

_____

_____

The Message of the Church Documents

Although the professional development of the teacher received minimal attention throughout Church literature on education (Appendixes A and B), what is mentioned is pregnant with meaning and implications for 21st-century teaching.

The *Declaration on Christian Education* advised Catholic school teachers to remain up to date in psychology, pedagogy, and the intellectual sciences. Excerpts from this document referencing the teacher with "a constant readiness to accept new ideas and to adapt the old" (Second Vatican Council, 1965/1988, #5); an awareness of "the advances in psychological, pedagogical and intellectual sciences" (#1) with a passion to excel in pedagogy; and an openness to the contemporary world depict the teacher as an innovator and collaborator with the secular educational community, once again exemplifying the new-paradigm thinking of Vatican II.

Lay Catholics in Schools: Witnesses to Faith warned that becoming outdated in pedagogical methods will "hinder them [teachers] severely in their call to contribute to an integral formation of the students" and "will also obscure the life witness that they must present" (Sacred Congregation for Catholic Education, 1982, #27). Document authors explained:

> Recent years have witnessed an extraordinary growth in science and technology; every object, situation, or value is subjected to a constant critical analysis. One effect is that our age is characterized by change; change that is constant and accelerated, that affects every last aspect of the human person and the society that he or she lives in. Because of change, knowledge that has been acquired and structures that have been established are quickly outdated; the need for new attitudes and new methods is constant. (#67)

As early as 1972, *To Teach as Jesus Did* exhorted Catholic school teachers to think futuristically about "new forms of schooling" and to become reflective practitioners who are committed to school improvement: "The search for new forms of schooling should . . . continue. . . . The point is that one must be open to the possibility that the school of the future, including the Catholic school, will in many ways be very different from the school of the past" (National Conference of Catholic Bishops, #124). The document also pointed out, "Catholic schools have the capacity and freedom to experiment. Administrators and teachers should therefore cooperate with parents in designing experimental models or pilot programs to improve educational standards and results" (#125).

Sharing the Light of Faith: National Catechetical Directory for Catholics of the United States invited teachers to collaborate with colleagues through "cooperative teaching." This teaching approach, "which cuts across the lines of particular disciplines, interdisciplinary curricula, team teaching, and the like help[s] to foster . . . goals of Catholic teaching" (National Conference of Catholic Bishops, 1979, #232). *Lay Catholics in Schools: Witnesses to Faith* iterated that the interior synthesis of the teacher, grounded in his or her spiritual and religious formation, "must be broadened and be kept up to date, on the same level as, and in harmony with, human formation as a whole" (Sacred Congregation for Catholic Education, 1982, #62). Thus, for the Catholic school teacher, professional competence consists in a combination of spiritual and human formation. The blend and balance of the teacher's interior synthesis with continual renewal and updating in the field of education constitutes the Catholic school teacher's ongoing, wholistic, formational commitment.

Implementing the Message

Since the Second Vatican Council, Catholic school teachers have been urged to continually renew, adapt, and update their knowledge in psychology, pedagogy, and the intellectual sciences. With the burst of advanced technologies that have marked the latter part of the 20th century, this need for continuous teacher renewal has become the status quo. It is obvious that the Catholic educator is called to be a lifelong learner in a way that is historically unprecedented.

Educators, in the main, are experiencing innovations in curriculum and instruction. Remaining updated implies remaining abreast of—

- **Innovative teaching strategies**, such as team-building and cooperative-learning strategies, teaching techniques that promote higher-order student thinking, and methodologies that teach children conflict-resolution skills
- **Technologies**, such as computers integrated into curricula, video, telecommunications, the Internet, CD-ROM, teleconferencing, and distance learning
- **Alternative assessment methods**, such as portfolios, product- and performance-based assessment, and other qualitative methods, to complement existing quantitative methodologies and thereby contribute breadth and depth to teachers' assessment of students

As a professional, the Catholic school teacher is additionally challenged to infuse the Christian/Catholic dimension throughout his or her teaching. This will be addressed in greater detail in the next section. A productive activity to conduct with fellow faculty members is to brainstorm ways that this can be done in each of the subject areas.

QUESTIONS FOR REFLECTION

1. *How readily do I adapt to change? What might be the reason(s) for my readiness or resistance in this area?*

_____

_____

_____

_____

_____

_____

_____

_____

2. *What knowledge and skill domains will my students need to be successful in a 21st-century world?*

_____

_____

_____

_____

_____

_____

_____

_____

3. *What knowledge and skill domains do I need to acquire to assist my students in their successful entry into a 21st-century world?*

_____

_____

_____

_____

_____

_____

_____

(Continued)

4. *What is my level of openness to faculty inservices? What is the reason for this?*

_____

_____

_____

_____

_____

_____

_____

_____

5. *What is the value of reflecting on my teaching practices?*

_____

_____

_____

_____

_____

_____

_____

_____

6. *The following is an example of how self-reflection has improved my teaching effectiveness:*

_____

_____

_____

_____

_____

_____

_____

_____

Teacher Resources

Brooks, J. G., & Brooks, M. G. (1993). *The case for constructivist classrooms.* Alexandria, VA: Association for Supervision and Curriculum Development.

Cetron, M., & Gayle, M. (1991). *Educational renaissance: Our schools at the turn of the twenty-first century.* New York: St. Martin's Press.

Dickinson, D. (Ed.). (1991). *Creating the future: Perspectives on educational change.* Aston Clinton, Bucks, UK: Accelerated Learning Systems Ltd.

Fried, R. L. (1995). *The passionate teacher: Practical guide.* Boston: Beacon Press.

Goodlad, J., Soder, R., & Sirotnik, K. (Eds.). (1990). *The moral dimensions of teaching.* San Francisco: Jossey-Bass.

Gunter, M. A., Estes, T. H., & Schwab, J. (1995). *Instruction: A models approach.* Boston: Allyn & Bacon.

LePage, A. (1987). *Transforming education: The new 3 R's*. Oakland: Oakmore House Press.

Papert, S. (1993). *The children's machine: Rethinking school in the age of the computer*. New York: Basic Books.

Sizer, T. R. (1992). *Horace's school: Redesigning the American high school*. New York: Houghton Mifflin.

Thornburg, D. (1992). *Edutrends 2010: Restructuring, technology, and the future of education*. San Carlos, CA: Starsong Publications.

Professional Journals

Catholic Education: A Journal of Inquiry and Practice
University of Dayton
300 College Park
Dayton, OH 45469-0510
(Jointly published by the University of Dayton, Saint Louis University, Fordham University, and the University of San Francisco)

Educational Leadership
Association for Supervision and
 Curriculum Development
1250 N. Pitt Street
Alexandria, VA 22314-9719

Momentum
National Catholic Educational Association
1077 30th Street, N.W., Suite 100
Washington, DC 20007-3852

Phi Delta Kappan
P. O. Box 789
Bloomington, IN 47402-9961

Teacher as Committed to Students' Spiritual Formation

TEACHER SELF-INVENTORY

Students' Spiritual Formation

Directions: For a self-evaluation of your commitment to your students' spiritual formation, complete the following items. For each item enter the number that most closely depicts the frequency of your experience. Enter your scores on page 66 to create a personal profile.

	Consistently 4	Often 3	Seldom 2	Never 1
As a Catholic school educator:				
1. Do I actively promote the values of religious education with my students?	___	___	___	___
2. Do I promote the moral development of my students through the use of specific methods, e.g., role-playing moral dilemmas, class meetings, discussions, questioning strategies?	___	___	___	___
3. Do I participate with my students in schoolwide prayer, e.g., liturgies and paraliturgies?	___	___	___	___
4. Do I help my students to create an atmosphere of reverence around the things of God?	___	___	___	___
5. Do I employ a variety of techniques to promote and to individualize the spiritual formation of my students?	___	___	___	___
6. Do I create a holy space (e.g., crucifix, icon, posters) in my classroom?	___	___	___	___
7. Do I create holy time (e.g., prayer, silent reflection) in my classroom with my students?	___	___	___	___
8. Do I engage in meaningful conversation beyond the scope of instruction with my students?	___	___	___	___
9. Do I assist my students in being aware of the countercultural aspects of the Christian lifestyle?	___	___	___	___
10. Am I willing to adjust a lesson in order to deal with a pressing class issue or to pursue a spiritual, religious, or morally based topic with my students?	___	___	___	___

Total: _____ = ____ + ____ + ____ + ____

• *Areas in which I am most proud of the spiritual formation of my students:*

_____
_____
_____
_____
_____
_____
_____
_____
_____
_____

• *Areas in which I could improve the spiritual formation of my students:*

_____
_____
_____
_____
_____
_____
_____
_____
_____
_____

The Message of the Church Documents

In 1972, the National Conference of Catholic Bishops defined the threefold purpose of Christian education in the acclaimed document *To Teach as Jesus Did*. The Catholic school teacher's mission consisted in the integration of three components into his or her teaching: Christian message, community, and service. In fact, the *distinguishing feature* of a Catholic school, according to this document, was "its commitment to the threefold purpose of Christian education" (#106). In 1979, through the document *Sharing the Light of Faith: National Catechetical Directory for Catholics of the United States*, the threefold purpose of Christian education was expanded to include a fourth dimension, that of worship. "It is . . . widely recognized that Catholic schools are to be communities of faith in which the Christian message, the experience of community, worship, and social concern are integrated in the total experience of students, their parents, and members of the faculty" (National Conference of Catholic Bishops, #9).

Three closely related themes predominate throughout the Church documents on education that help to expand upon the religious dimension of the Catholic school: (a) the integration throughout the curriculum of religious truth and values with the lives and cultures of the students, (b) the promotion of the spiritual and religious formation and transformation of students, and (c) the instilling of an appreciation for Christian service in students. Let us examine the evolution of each of these three themes over the past 30-plus years of Church documentation.

Integrating Religious Truth and Values with Life. The concept of integrating throughout the curriculum religious truth and values with life was briefly mentioned in the 1965 document *Declaration on Christian Education*. The teacher was advised to orient "the whole of human culture to the message of salvation that the knowledge which the pupils acquire of the world, of life and of man is illumined by faith" (Second Vatican Council 1965/1988, #8). In 1972, with the publication by the National Conference of Catholic Bishops of *To Teach as Jesus Did*, this sophisticated ideology took root, manifesting additional layers of meaning:

> This integration of religious truth and values with life distinguishes the Catholic school from other schools. This is a matter of crucial importance today in view of contemporary trends and pressures to compartmentalize life and learning and to isolate the religious dimension of existence from other areas of human life. (#105)

> It [instruction in religious truth and values] is not one more subject alongside the rest, but instead it is perceived and functions as the underlying reality in which the student's experiences of learning and living achieve their coherence and their deepest meaning. (#103)

> The Catholic school is the unique setting within which this ideal can be realized in the lives of Catholic children and young people. Only in such a school can they experience learning and living fully integrated in the light of faith. (#102-103)

Clearly, every aspect of school life becomes an opportunity for linking truth and values with life; the curriculum extends beyond the scope of academic subjects into extracurricular religious and social activities.

The 1977 document *The Catholic School* further expanded this concept. In summary, it identified the task of the Catholic school as

> fundamentally a synthesis of culture and faith, and a synthesis of faith and life: the first is reached by integrating all the different aspects of human knowledge through the subjects taught, in the light of the Gospel; the second in the growth of the virtues characteristic of the Christian. (Sacred Congregation for Catholic Education, #37)

Thus, according to the document authors, the purpose of academic subjects is "not merely the attainment of knowledge but the acquisition of values and the discovery of truth" (#39). A well-rounded education, the document noted, must of necessity instill a religious dimension throughout the curriculum, for "religion is an effective contribution to the development of other aspects of a personality in the measure in which it is integrated into general education" (#19). This important approach to education "takes place in the school in the form of personal contacts and commitments which consider absolute values in a life-context and seek to insert them into a life-framework" (#27).

The function and power of the teacher in this context are awe inspiring, as validated by the following excerpts from *The Catholic School* (Sacred Congregation for Catholic Education, 1977): "When the Christian teacher helps a pupil to grasp, appreciate and assimilate these values, he is guiding him towards eternal realities. This movement towards the Uncreated Source of all knowledge highlights the importance of teaching for the growth of faith" (#42); "The teacher can form the mind and heart of his pupils and guide them to develop a total commitment to Christ, with their whole personality enriched by human culture" (#40); and "A teacher who is full of Christian wisdom, well prepared in his own subject, does more than convey the sense of what he is teaching to his pupils. Over and above what he says, he guides his pupils beyond his mere words to the heart of total Truth" (#41).

New-paradigm thinking reached a pinnacle in this theme of linking truth and values with the life of the student. In fact, a theology of teaching began to take root here. Maria Harris (1987), in her reflections upon the writings of theologian Martin Buber, shed light upon this area:

Whenever I reread Martin Buber's classic essay on education, it is this last rendering of subject that captures my attention. Buber speaks of the educator discovering an inner religious impulse to be in the service of the One who is able to do what human beings cannot do: to create and form and transform. The educator is set in the *imitatio Dei absconditi sed non ignoti*: the imitation of the divinity who, although hidden from sight, is not unknown. Once more we are met by the holiness of teaching. From the attitude of contemplation, we discover that the teacher is—through engagement with subject matter in all its renderings—someone called by, called with, and calling upon the Creator God to save, to perfect, and to manifest the divine image that dwells by reason of subjectivity in all existing beings. (pp. 33-34)

Sharing the Light of Faith: National Catechetical Directory for Catholics of the United States concretized this idea of integrating subject matter with religious truth and values:

Belief can also be expressed in the visual arts, in poetry and literature, in music and architecture, in philosophy, and scientific or technological achievements. These, too, can be signs of God's presence, continuations of His creative activity, instruments by which believers glorify Him and give witness to the world concerning the faith that is in them. (National Conference of Catholic Bishops, 1979, #59)

The Religious Dimension of Education in a Catholic School further emphasized and elaborated on the integration of the religious dimension into academic areas. Declaring that "the Catholic school . . . is based on an educational philosophy in which faith, culture and life are brought into harmony" (Congregation for Catholic Education, 1988, #34), it proceeded to state that the academics are stimulated by new perspectives when integrated with a religious dimension. For example, in the study of science, the universe "is given new significance when seen with the eyes of faith" (#51). The document stated further:

Within the overall process of education, special mention must be made of the intellectual work done by students. Although Christian life consists in loving God and doing his will, intellectual work is intimately involved. The light of Christian faith stimulates a desire to know the universe as God's creation. It enkindles a love for the truth that will not be satisfied with superficiality in knowledge or judgment. It awakens a critical sense which examines statements rather than accepting them blindly. It impels the mind to learn with careful order and precise methods, and to work with a sense of responsibility. It provides the strength needed to accept the sacrifices and the perseverance required by intellectual labor. When fatigued, the Christian student remembers the command of Genesis and the invitation of the Lord. (#49)

To present subject matter without the religious dimension is to provide a fragmented and inadequate curriculum. As *The Religious Dimension of Education in a Catholic School* pointed out, in addition to the educators who teach science, technology, history, art, and literature, "teachers dealing with areas such as anthropology, biology, psychology, sociology and philosophy all have the opportunity to present a complete picture of the human person . . . " (Congregation for Catholic Education, 1988, #55). Educating to the whole child in any subject area intimately involves the integration of the religious dimension.

Continuing to expand this concept to include the dimension of mystery, *The Religious Dimension of Education in a Catholic School* stated: "Students learn many things about the human person by studying science; but science has nothing to say about mystery. Teachers should help students begin to discover the mystery within the human person . . . " (Congregation for Catholic Education, 1988, #76). Parker Palmer (1985) further illuminated this sublime aspect of Christian education:

In Christian tradition, truth is not a concept that "works" but an incarnation that lives. The "Word" our knowledge seeks is not a verbal construct but a reality in history and the flesh. Christian tradition understands truth to be embodied in personal terms, the terms of one who said, "I am the way, and the truth, and the life." Where conventional education deals with abstract and impersonal facts and theories, an education shaped by Christian spirituality draws us toward incarnate and personal truth. In this education we come to know the world not simply as an objectified system of empirical objects in logical connection with each other, but as an organic body of personal relations and responses, a living and evolving community of creativity and compassion. Education of this sort means more than teaching the facts and learning the reasons so we can manipulate life toward our ends. It means being drawn into personal responsiveness and accountability to each other and the world of which we are a part. (pp. 14-15)

The Religious Dimension of Education in a Catholic School claimed that, deprived of an education containing this dimension, students sadly "run the risk of living the best years of their lives at a shallow level" (Congregation for Catholic Education, 1988, #48). Hence, an interdisciplinary approach to teaching was endorsed within this document:

Interdisciplinary work has been introduced into Catholic schools with positive results, for there are questions and topics that are not easily treated within the limitations of a single subject area. Religious themes should be included; they arise naturally when dealing with topics such as the human person, society, or history. (#64)

By the same token, this 1988 document cautioned that a "Catholic school . . . would no longer deserve the title if, no matter how good its reputation for teaching in other areas, there were just grounds for a reproach of negligence or deviation in religious education properly so-called" (#66).

Promoting the Spiritual and Religious Formation and Transformation of Students.
The second theme to expand upon the religious dimension of the Catholic school is that of the teacher promoting the spiritual and religious formation and transformation of students. In the document *Declaration on Christian Education*, directives to the Catholic school teacher included that the students: "acquire gradually a more perfect sense of responsibility in the proper development of their own lives" and "be stimulated to make sound moral judgments based on a well-formed conscience" (Second Vatican Council, 1965/1988, #1); be introduced to the mystery of salvation, the life of Christ, and the gift of faith; strive toward justice and truth; be hopeful; and learn how to worship God.

The Catholic School reminded teachers of the essential component that distinguishes the Catholic school from others: "It is precisely in the Gospel of Christ, taking root in the minds and lives of the faithful, that the Catholic school finds its definition . . ." (Sacred Congregation for Catholic Education, 1977, #9). The document stated further:

In Him [Jesus Christ] the Catholic school differs from all others which limit themselves to forming men. Its task is to form Christian men, and, by its teaching and witness, show non-Christians something of the mystery of Christ Who surpasses all human understanding. (#47)

This document offered hints of a methodology for instilling the Gospel message in students. By encouraging students' self-reflection, by nurturing their freedom of inquiry, and by sensitizing their consciences to absolute human values, the teacher establishes a foundation from which an authentic Christian morality may emerge. The document asserted that the school "must help him [the student] spell out the meaning of his experiences and their truths. Any school which neglects this duty and which offers merely pre-cast conclusions hinders the personal development of its pupils" (#27). The document authors explained:

> It is one of the formal tasks of a school, as an institution for education, to draw out the ethical dimension for the precise purpose of arousing the individual's inner spiritual dynamism and to aid his achieving that moral freedom which complements the psychological. Behind this moral freedom, however, stand those absolute values which alone give meaning and value to human life. (#30)

Thus, the school, according to these authors, "must develop persons who are responsible and inner-directed, capable of choosing freely in conformity with their conscience" (#31).

Complementing this emphasis on the student's freedom of inquiry, *Lay Catholics in Schools: Witnesses to Faith* stated:

> Every school, and every educator in the school, ought to be striving "to form strong and responsible individuals, who are capable of making free and correct choices," thus preparing young people "to open themselves more and more to reality, and to form in themselves a clear idea of the meaning of life." (Sacred Congregation for Catholic Education, 1982, #17)

This formational process, the document warned, is never to be offered "coldly and abstractly" (#28), but rather as a gift, which emanates naturally from the person of the teacher and becomes incarnated in the person of the student, a unique opportunity for evangelization.

> The Catholic teacher, therefore, cannot be content simply to present Christian values as a set of abstract objectives to be admired, even if this be done positively and with imagination; they must be presented as values which generate human attitudes, and these attitudes must be encouraged in students. Examples of such attitudes would be these: a freedom which includes respect for others; conscientious responsibility; a sincere and constant search for truth; a calm and peaceful critical spirit; a spirit of solidarity with and service toward all other persons; a sensitivity for justice; a special awareness of being called to be positive agents of change in a society that is undergoing continuous transformation. (#30)

In regard to the actual teaching of religion, *The Religious Dimension of Education in a Catholic School* recommended the employment of the discovery method in one's teaching as an important methodology, which encourages the person of Jesus to come alive for students. This document acclaimed the ultimate goal of religious instruction to be experiential, that is, instruction that enables students to "see again the example of his [Jesus'] life, listen to his words, hear his invitation as addressed to them: 'Come to me, all of you'" (Congregation for Catholic Education, 1988, #74). The authors of this document proclaimed that an experiential understanding of ecclesiology and the sacraments would guarantee the growth of the religious dimension of students; accordingly, these authors advised that teachers "help students to discover the real value of the sacraments: they accompany the believer on his or her journey through life" (#78). Document authors stated further, "An understanding of the sacramental journey has profound educational implications. Students become aware that being a member of the Church is something dynamic, responding to every person's need to continue growing all through life" (#79).

New-paradigm thinking saturated *The Religious Dimension of Education in a Catholic School*. It encouraged the religious development of students to be realized through dynamic membership in the Church and to be spiritually evolving throughout their lifetime. This implies a religion curriculum that is personalized and participative. For example, reference is made to the sacrament of reconciliation as "not just a devotional practice, but rather a personal encounter with him [the Lord], through the mediation of his minister. After this celebration we can resume our journey with renewed strength and joy" (Congregation for Catholic Education, 1988, #93).

In regard to Christology, *The Religious Dimension of Education in a Catholic School* stated: "It is possible to love a person [Jesus]; it is rather difficult to love a formula" (Congregation for Catholic Education, 1988, #107). Authentic involvement, integrating meaningful religious instruction into the personal experience of the individual student, as opposed to the rote learning of doctrine and the rote performance of ritual, becomes the desired modus operandi of the post-Vatican II Christian. The document explained, "What characterizes a Catholic school, therefore, is that it guide students in such a way 'that the development of each one's own personality will be matched by the growth of that new creation which he or she became by baptism'" (#98). This process, the document authors pointed out, "might therefore be described as an organic set of elements with a single purpose: the gradual development of every capability of every student, enabling each one to attain an integral formation within a context that includes the Christian religious dimension and recognizes the help of grace" (#99).

Instilling an Appreciation for Christian Service in Students. In the *Declaration on Christian Education*, the teacher was urged to instill a sense of Christian service in students, to assist them in developing a global mind-set that promotes "the good of society in this world and for the development of a world more worthy of man" (Second Vatican Council, 1965/1988, #3). *Sharing the Light of Faith: National Catechetical Directory for Catholics of the United States* continued to define Christian service as "not only responding to needs when asked, but taking the initiative in seeking out the needs of individuals and communities, and encouraging students to do the same" (National Conference of Catholic Bishops, 1979, #210). This document suggested that students be gradually introduced to the notion of Christian service. Teaching concern for others in the elementary grades, in addition to studying the lives of the saints and other heroic contemporaries, may establish a foundation for service projects in the later grades.

Implementing the Message

Catholic educators are called to tell the *story* of Christian faith, which includes its scriptures, creeds, doctrines, theologies, sacraments, rituals, and so on. Beyond telling the story, however, they are called to educate the very beings of their students, "to inform, form, and transform . . . who they are and how they live—with the meaning and ethic of Christian faith" (Groome, 1996, p. 118). Hence, the story transforms into *vision* in the lives of students. Thomas Groome wrote, "Every teacher in a Catholic school, regardless of what discipline of learning he/she teaches, has umpteen teachable moments for mediating between the lives of students and Christian Story/Vision" (p. 118).

With the formulation of advanced teaching strategies during the past quarter-century, such as cooperative learning techniques, conflict-resolution models, synectics, and concept development models, as well as of a variety of technologies, the Catholic educator has at his or her disposal an abundance of methods and materials to enliven the teaching of religion. The most advanced teaching methodologies and technologies, however, can never substitute for a teacher lacking in his or her own spiritual formation. Teacher enthusiasm translates into student engagement. Only spiritually alive teachers can enliven the spiritualities of students.

Thom and Joani Schultz (1993), two Protestant educators, offered insightful descriptions of the teaching methodologies of Jesus. The following was extracted from their book *Why Nobody Learns Much of Anything at Church: And How to Fix It*, with minor adaptations.

JESUS' LEARNING TECHNIQUES

1. Start with the learner's context. Jesus used objects and story subjects that were familiar to his learners. Boats. Fish. Sheep. Water. Wine. Bread. He started where they were. He knew that effective learning builds upon what the learner already knows. . . . What are the familiar tools of a group of third-graders? Toys! We can use these tools—as Jesus did—to help kids learn from their own context. What are familiar symbols for older students? Car keys. Sports objects. Use these icons, as Jesus did, to assist your students to learn from their own context. Bring these items into your classrooms as visual learning tools.

Starting with the learner's context emphasizes learning, not teaching.

2. Allow learners to discover truth. Jesus beckoned Peter to walk on the water—to learn about faith. Peter discovered a bit of truth through his own experience. Jesus could have simply lectured Peter about faith, but he wanted Peter to discover.

People learn best when they discover answers for themselves. In discovery learning, the teacher steps away from being the prime dispenser of answers and becomes more of a coach and facilitator.

If we're more interested in teaching, we can tell our class how God's power and creativity are present in nature. But if we're more interested in learning, we'll take the class outside and let them discover God's handiwork.

With discovery learning, the emphasis is on learning, not teaching.

3. Take advantage of teachable moments. The woman caught in adultery, the storm on the lake, the paralytic in the synagogue. Jesus knew when his learners were ripe for learning. He never hesitated to create a lesson out of what happened around him. In contrast to the rote practices of the Pharisees, Jesus knew the difference between teaching and learning. When he observed people engaged in a captivating activity, he knew they were ready to learn, and he took advantage of the opportunity.

In the teaching of religion, we can accept that our learners will learn little if they're uninterested or bored. When they're truly captivated by something, they're already learning.

When seizing teachable moments, the emphasis is on learning, not teaching.

4. Provide learners with opportunities to practice what they've learned. Jesus instructed the rich man, then challenged him to sell all his possessions. Jesus taught his disciples about betrayal, then gave Peter, Judas, and the others time to practice their loyalty. Their failures seared the lesson into their memories.

Allowing learners to practice what they've learned puts the emphasis on learning, not teaching.

(Adapted with permission from *Why Nobody Learns Much of Anything at Church: And How to Fix It*, 1993, published by Group Publishing, Inc., Loveland, CO.)

Religious instruction should challenge student thinking beyond the recall and comprehension levels and into higher-order thinking levels of application, analysis, synthesis, and evaluation. It is at these higher-order levels that students take ownership of concepts that become relevant to their lives. Moreover, religious instruction should be designed to teach to the different learning styles of students. One way to accomplish this is through a multiple-intelligences approach to instructional design, which will be discussed in the next section (see pp. 60-61). As teachers design instruction to promote the higher-order thinking of students as well as to address their varied learning styles, they simultaneously stimulate the students' use of their imagination. Lower-order thinking, which is the basis of, and necessity for, analytic and creative thinking, too often constitutes deficient learning and student irrelevance. It is through the use of the imagination that students are able to conceive of, and relate to, the divine. Therefore, teachers should encourage students to use their imagination in religious instruction through guided meditations, storytelling, art activities, creative writing, moral dilemmas, drama, and other creative involvements.

The following is a sample of a guided meditation designed to fully involve younger students in a prayer experience. It was offered by Gwen Costello (1991) in an article entitled "Meeting Jesus Face to Face." She described this exercise to her students as a "prayer of imagination."

> Close your eyes . . . take a deep breath . . . and relax . . . There is a garden . . . a special garden . . . It is a place where Mary of Magdala was looking for Jesus after his resurrection . . . Walk into this garden . . . Feel the cool, soft grass tickle your feet as you walk . . . There are many beautiful shade trees here . . . Sit comfortably under a tree and look around the garden. It is filled with colorful flowers . . . pink and purple ones . . . white lilies . . . yellow daisies . . . Breathe in deeply and smell the sweetness of all these flowers.

> Someone is standing behind you . . . turn around and see that it is Jesus . . . He smiles at you . . . calls you by name . . . and reaches out his hand to help you up . . . Jesus hugs you . . . His arms around you feel strong and protective . . . "Come," Jesus tells you . . . and he places his arm around your shoulders and leads you to a large tree beside the creek . . . Sit under the tree next to Jesus . . . Feel how good it is to be here with him.

> What would you like to say to Jesus? . . . What would you like him to say to you? You will now have a short time to converse with him, to share your deepest feelings with him . . . (allow a minute) . . . It is now time to say good-bye to Jesus, knowing that you can converse with him in this way anytime you wish. Say good-bye to Jesus . . . he smiles and waves to you . . . open your eyes and return to the room.

QUESTIONS FOR REFLECTION

1. *In what specific ways does my school reflect a fourfold commitment to Christian education through:*

*Christian message?*_____
_____
_____
_____
_____
_____
_____
_____

Community? _____
_____
_____
_____
_____
_____
_____

Service? _____
_____
_____
_____
_____
_____
_____

Worship? _____
_____
_____
_____
_____
_____
_____

2. *In what ways is my school outstanding in one or more of the above areas?*

    _____

    _____

    _____

    _____

    _____

    _____

    _____

    _____

3. *In what ways could my school improve in one or more of the above areas?*

    _____

    _____

    _____

    _____

    _____

    _____

    _____

    _____

4. *Beyond the scope of the religion class, do I integrate religious truths and values into other instructional areas?*

    _____

    _____

    _____

    _____

    _____

    _____

    _____

5. *The following is an example of how I incorporate religious truths and values into my instruction:*

    _____

    _____

    _____

    _____

    _____

    _____

    _____

6. *How do I assess whether my students are grasping these religious truths and values?*

_____

_____

_____

_____

_____

_____

_____

_____

7. *If I do not integrate religious truth and values into my instructional areas, what can I do to enrich my teaching with a religious dimension?*

_____

_____

_____

_____

_____

_____

_____

_____

8. *The following is an example of how I have promoted freedom of inquiry among my students and have encouraged them to reflect upon truths internal to their experiences:*

_____

_____

_____

_____

_____

_____

_____

9. *What methodologies do I employ in the actual teaching of religion?*

_____

_____

_____

_____

_____

_____

_____

10. *The following is an example of how I promote the moral development of my students:*

_____

_____

_____

_____

_____

_____

_____

_____

Teacher Resources

Coles, R. (1990). *The spiritual life of children.* Boston: Houghton Mifflin.

DeVillers, S. (1994). *Lectionary-based catechesis for children: A catechist's guide.* New York: Paulist Press.

Donze, M. T. (1982). *In my heart room: Sixteen love prayers for little children.* Liguori, MO: Liguori Publications.

Donze, M. T. (1985). *Touching a child's heart: An innovative, encouraging guide to becoming a good storyteller.* Notre Dame, IN: Ave Maria Press.

Halverson, D. (1989). *Teaching prayer in the classroom.* Nashville: Abingdon Press.

Halverson, D. (1992). *New ways to tell the old, old story.* Nashville: Abingdon Press.

Hawker, J. (1985). *Catechetics in the Catholic school.* Washington, DC: National Catholic Educational Association.

Lickona, T. (1983). *Raising good children.* New York: Bantam Books.

Lickona, T. (1991). *Educating for character: How our schools can teach respect and responsibility.* New York: Bantam Books.

Manternach, J. (1989). *A practical book for prayerful catechists—And the children pray.* Notre Dame, IN: Ave Maria Press.

Manternach, J., & Pfeifer, C. J. (1991). *Creative catechist.* Mystic, CT: Twenty-Third Publications.

Mathson, P. (1992). *Creativities: 101 creative activities for children to celebrate God's love, for kindergarten through sixth grade.* Notre Dame, IN: Ave Maria Press.

McBride, A. A. (1976). *Creative teaching in Christian education.* Boston: Allyn & Bacon.

Ozar, L. A. (1994). *Creating a curriculum that works.* Washington, DC: National Catholic Educational Association.

Ozar, L. A. (1995). *"By their fruits you shall know them . . . ": K-12 religious education outcomes for Catholic schools.* Washington, DC: National Catholic Educational Association.

Reehorst, J. (1986). *Guided meditations for children.* Dubuque, IA: William C. Brown.

Sork, D. A., Boyd, D., & Sedano, M. (1981). *The catechist formation book.* New York: Paulist Press.

Traviss, M. P. (1985). *Student moral development in the Catholic school.* Washington, DC: National Catholic Educational Association.

Treston, K. (1993). *A new vision of religious education.* Mystic, CT: Twenty-Third Publications.

Periodicals

Catechist. Peter Li, Inc., Dayton, OH (1-800-543-4383)
The Catechist's Connection. The National Catholic Reporter Publishing Co., Inc., Kansas City, MO (1-800-444-8910)
Religion Teacher's Journal. Twenty-Third Publications, Mystic, CT (1-800-321-0411)

Videos Recommended by Media Center Directors
(From Final Report of a National Study of Catholic Religious Education/Catechesis, 1994)

First Eucharist (for Children)
> *A Child's First Communion*, Liguori Publications
> *Grandma's Bread*, Franciscan Communications

First Penance (Sacrament of Reconciliation for Children)
> *A Child's First Penance*, Ligouri Publications
> *Skateboard*, Franciscan Communications

Confirmation (Jr. High/High School)
> *The Choice*, Franciscan Communications
> *Confirmation: It's Your Choice*, Ligouri Publications

Marriage (High School)
> *Issues in Sexuality/Marriage: A Life Long Commitment*, Brown-ROA
> *Your Marriage*, Ligouri Publications
> *Helping Young People Get Ready for Marriage*, Tabor

Christian Sexuality (Grades 5-6)
> *In God's Image*, Franciscan Publications
> *Teens and Chastity*, Molly Kelly/Center for Learning

Scripture (Jr. High)
> *The Bible: What's It All About?* Franciscan Communications

Catholic Social Teaching (Senior High/Adult)
> *Bring Down the Walls*, United States Catholic Conference
> *The Mouse's Tale*, Catholic Relief Services
> *Romero*, Paulist Pictures

The Church—Its Mission and Work (Senior High/Adult)
> *Church and Ministry*, Tabor
> *What Catholics Believe*, Ligouri Publications
> *Vatican II*, Hallel Communications

Overall Best Video for Use with Jr. High/High School Students
> *Pardon and Peace*, Franciscan Communications
> *Teens and Chastity*, Molly Kelly/Center for Learning
> *Don Kimball and Friends*, Tabor

Overall Best Video for Use with Middle-Grade Students (Grades 3-6)
> *McGee and Me*, ECU/Tyndale House
> *Sacred Heart Kids Club Series*, Sacred Heart Sisters

THEME FIVE:

Teacher as Committed to Students' Human Development

TEACHER SELF-INVENTORY

Students' Human Development

Directions: For a self-evaluation of your commitment to your students' human development, complete the following items. For each item enter the number that most closely depicts the frequency of your experience. Enter your scores on page 66 to create a personal profile.

	Consistently 4	Often 3	Seldom 2	Never 1
As a Catholic school educator:				
1. Do I design my curriculum to accommodate the diverse learning styles of my students?	____	____	____	____
2. Do I maintain high, but realistic, academic standards for my students?	____	____	____	____
3. Do I personalize my curriculum so that my students may relate subject-matter content to their lived experiences?	____	____	____	____
4. Do I assess my students in multiple ways?	____	____	____	____
5. Do I encourage my students to learn beyond the levels of recall and comprehension?	____	____	____	____
6. Do I provide opportunities for my students to apply, analyze, synthesize, and evaluate information?	____	____	____	____
7. Do I encourage my students to utilize technology?	____	____	____	____
8. Do I strive to understand at ever-deeper levels the stages of child development and how these stages relate to my teaching and my students' learning?	____	____	____	____
9. Do I promote learning strategies with my students that will empower them to become lifelong learners who will become functional in a highly technological world?	____	____	____	____
10. Do I provide opportunities for my students to express and develop their creativity?	____	____	____	____

Total: _____ = _____ + _____ + _____ + _____

● *Areas in which I am most proud of the human development of my students:*

_____
_____
_____
_____
_____
_____
_____
_____
_____
_____

● *Areas in which I could improve the human development of my students:*

_____
_____
_____
_____
_____
_____
_____
_____
_____
_____

The Message of the Church Documents

Like Theme Three, which delineated the professional development of the teacher, the human development of students received minimal focus throughout the Church literature on education (see Appendixes A and B). In a similar fashion, however, statements made are potent with contemporary meaning.

In 1965, the *Declaration on Christian Education* urged educators to teach to the whole child. In 1977, *The Catholic School* elucidated this concept by stating that this meant "helping to provide every child with an education that respects his complete development . . . " (Sacred Congregation for Catholic Education, #82). The authors of this document wisely advised:

> Precisely because the [Catholic] school endeavors to answer the needs of a society characterized by depersonalization and a mass production mentality which so easily result from scientific and technological development, it must develop into an authentically formational school, reducing such risks to a minimum. (#31)

An "authentically formational school" personalizes the learning experiences of students; that is, it meets the unique needs and capabilities of individual students and, at the same time, equips them with high academic standards. The task of the teacher extends well beyond the mere transmission of knowledge. Educating to the whole child reinforces the notion of integral education, as described in *Lay Catholics in Schools: Witnesses to Faith*:

> In virtue of its mission, then, the school must be concerned with constant and careful attention to cultivating in students the intellectual, creative, and aesthetic faculties of the human person;

to develop in them the ability to make correct use of their judgment, will, and affectivity; to promote in them a sense of values; to encourage just attitudes and prudent behavior; to introduce them to the cultural patrimony handed down from previous generations; to prepare them for professional life, and to encourage the friendly interchange among students of diverse cultures and backgrounds that will lead to mutual understanding. (Sacred Congregation for Catholic Education, 1982, #12)

In *To Teach as Jesus Did*, teachers were advised to prepare students to become lifelong learners: "Today, perhaps more than ever before, it is important to recognize that learning is a lifelong experience. Rapid, radical changes in contemporary society demand well planned, continuing efforts to assimilate new data, new insights, new modes of thinking and acting" (National Conference of Catholic Bishops, 1972, #43). Additionally, authors of this document urged Catholic school teachers to prepare students in the ethical use of technology:

Technology is one of the most marvelous expressions of the human spirit in history; but it is not an unmixed blessing. It can enrich life immeasurably or make a tragedy of life. The choice is man's, and education has a powerful role in shaping that choice. (#33)

Implementing the Message

Catholic educators are specially called to address the whole child. In fact, the Church document of 1977, *The Catholic School*, specifically stated, "The school must begin from the principle that its educational program is intentionally directed to the growth of the whole person . . . since in Christ . . . all human values find their fulfillment and unity. Herein lies the specifically Catholic character of the school" (#29). But, what constitutes the "whole person"? There is a variety of responses to this question in the educational world. Traditionally, teachers have been aware of visual, auditory, and kinesthetic learners. A more recent approach has been offered by Howard Gardner (1983), a research psychologist and professor of neurology at Harvard University, who has suggested multiple intelligence theory as a wider lens through which to achieve an understanding of each student's learning style. His theory claims that there are seven areas of the brain that support seven ways of knowing: logical-mathematical, linguistic, spatial, musical, bodily-kinesthetic, interpersonal, and intrapersonal. In his work *Gifts of the Spirit: Multiple Intelligences*, Ronald Nuzzi (1996, pp. 10-18) described and discussed each intelligence. His descriptions are adapted below in Table 3.

Table 3: The Multiple Intelligences	
Logical-Mathematical	Uses numbers correctly and effectively and uses reason to solve problems
Linguistic	Uses words and language effectively
Spatial	Perceives the physical world clearly and is able to think in images, pictures, and mental illustrations
Musical	Perceives and expresses variations in rhythm, pitch, and melody
Bodily-Kinesthetic	Uses the body to express ideas and feelings and to perform certain valuable functions; manipulates and handles objects skillfully
Interpersonal	Understands, perceives, and appreciates the feelings and moods of others
Intrapersonal	Understands one's own self; perceives accurately one's strengths and weaknesses and draws on this understanding as a means to direct one's actions

Data from studies done in the fields of psychology and neurobiology support the correspondence between regions of the brain and these forms of cognition. Individuals are usually dominant in two or three of these intelligences.

Traditional education has addressed predominantly the logical-mathematical and linguistic intelligences. The question stands before Catholic educators: "Do we in Catholic education, who are committed to teaching to the whole child, address other areas of intelligence?" Moreover, Catholic pedagogy demands that religious truth and values be interwoven throughout the curriculum, forming the foundation of all instruction. Traditional assessment methods address the logical-mathematical and linguistic areas. In order to adequately assess the other areas of cognition, alternative (qualitative) assessment methods must be employed; to do otherwise conveys a mixed message that gives prominence to logical and linguistic cognition. This presents a formidable challenge to the Catholic school teacher, one that extends well beyond that of transmitting a body of information to students. To teach to the whole child requires a teacher who is ministerial, who individualizes instruction to the needs of each child.

QUESTIONS FOR REFLECTION

1. *In what ways do I address the affective (emotional) domains of my students?*

_____

_____

_____

_____

_____

_____

_____

_____

2. *The following is an example of how I encourage my students to learn in ways beyond the linguistic and the logical-mathematical intelligences:*

_____

_____

_____

_____

_____

_____

_____

_____

(Continued)

3. *When encouraging my students to learn in ways other than the linguistic and the logical-mathematical intelligences, what alternative methods do I employ to assess their performance?*

_____

_____

_____

_____

_____

_____

_____

_____

_____

4. *What is my greatest frustration in attempting to meet the learning needs of my students?*

_____

_____

_____

_____

_____

_____

_____

_____

_____

5. *What is my greatest satisfaction in attempting to address the learning needs of my students?*

_____

_____

_____

_____

_____

_____

_____

_____

_____

6. *What are the enriching usages of technology in my school? in my classroom?*

_____

_____

_____

_____

_____

_____

_____

_____

Teacher Resources

Armstrong, T. (1987). *In their own way: Discovering and encouraging your child's personal learning style.* Los Angeles: Jeremy P. Tarcher.

Armstrong, T. (1992). *Seven kinds of smart: Discovering and using your natural intelligence.* New York: New American Library/Penguin.

Forte, I., & Schurr, S. (1995). *Making portfolios, products, and performances meaningful and manageable for students and teachers.* Nashville: Incentive Publications.

Harmin, M. (1994). *Inspiring active learning.* Alexandria, VA: Association for Supervision and Curriculum Development.

Healy, J. M. (1987). *Your child's growing mind: A guide to learning and brain development from birth to adolescence.* New York: Doubleday.

Healy, J. M. (1990). *Endangered minds: Why our children don't think.* New York: Simon & Schuster.

Lazear, D. (1991). *Seven ways of knowing: Teaching for multiple intelligences.* Palatine, IL: Skylight.

Lazear, D. (1991). *Seven ways of teaching: The artistry of teaching with multiple intelligences.* Palatine, IL: Skylight.

Lazear, D. (1994). *Multiple intelligence approaches to assessment: Solving the assessment conundrum.* Tucson, AZ: Zephyr Press.

Thornburg, D. (1989). *The role of technology in teaching to the whole child: Multiple intelligences in the classroom.* San Carlos, CA: Starsong Publications.

Wiggins, G. P. (1993). *Assessing student performance.* San Francisco, CA: Jossey-Bass.

Conclusion

The invitation "to teach as Jesus did" is a call to ministry of the highest caliber. It is no ordinary invitation to teaching. The Catholic response to this invitation is wholistic, involving the simultaneous, ongoing formation of the teacher and student in the context of subject matter, with subject matter based in religious truth and values. Each of the components mentioned previously—the teacher as a community builder, committed to lifelong spiritual and professional growth as well as to the students' spiritual and human development—cannot operate independently. They have been discussed separately for purposes of analysis and understanding.

There must be a synergy of these components, however, in which the ongoing result is the Catholic school teacher who contributes to the transformation of students, patiently shepherding them closer to the light of the divine. As Catholic educators increase participation in a shared identity, Catholic education will increasingly become a beacon of hope and stability for 21st-century humanity.

ASSESSMENT OF YOUR EFFECTIVENESS
AS A CATHOLIC SCHOOL EDUCATOR

A.   **From each of the teacher self-inventories taken in the preceding chapters, insert your total score:**

1. Community Building   *Total:*   _____

2. Lifelong Spiritual Growth   *Total:*   _____

3. Lifelong Professional Development   *Total:*   _____

4. Students' Spiritual Formation   *Total:*   _____

5. Students' Human Development   *Total:*   _____

B.   **Apply your scores to the following graph by shading in each category horizontally.**

Teacher as:								
COMMUNITY BUILDER								
COMMITTED TO LIFELONG SPIRITUAL GROWTH								
COMMITTED TO LIFELONG PROFESSIONAL DEVELOPMENT								
PROMOTING STUDENTS' SPIRITUAL FORMATION								
PROMOTING STUDENTS' HUMAN DEVELOPMENT								
	10 **15** **20** **25** **30** **35** **40**							
	Ineffective **Very Effective**							

QUESTIONS FOR REFLECTION

1. *According to your profile, what is your overall effectiveness as a Catholic school educator?*

_____

_____

_____

_____

_____

_____

_____

_____

2. *Is this an accurate reflection of your overall effectiveness as a Catholic school teacher? Why or why not?*

_____

_____

_____

_____

_____

_____

_____

_____

3. *What areas indicate your strengths? your weaknesses?*

_____

_____

_____

_____

_____

_____

_____

4. *How might you improve your weak areas?*

_____

_____

_____

_____

_____

_____

_____

5. *How might you continue to improve your strong areas?*

    _____
    _____
    _____
    _____
    _____
    _____
    _____
    _____

6. *What insights have you derived from this process?*

    _____
    _____
    _____
    _____
    _____
    _____
    _____
    _____

"But the Greatest of These Is Love"

Though I teach with skill
Of the finest teachers
And have not love,
I am only a clever speaker and charming entertainer.
And though I understand all techniques and try many methods,
And though I have much training, so that I feel competent,
But have no understanding of the way my students think and feel,
It is not enough.

And if I spend many hours in preparation
And become tense and nervous with the strain,
But have no love and understanding
Of the personal problems of my students,
It still is not enough.

The loving teacher is very patient, very kind;
Is not shocked when people bring him or her their confidences;
Does not gossip; is not easily discouraged;
Does not behave in ways that are unworthy,
But is at all times a living example to his or her students
Of the good way of life of which he or she speaks.
Love never fails.

But, whether there be materials, they shall become obsolete;
Whether there be methods, they shall become outmoded;
Whether there be techniques, they shall be abandoned;
For we know only a little,
And can pass on to our students only a little;
But, when we have love
Then all our efforts will become creative,
And our influence will live forever
In the lives of our students.

And now abide skill, methods, love,
These three;
But the greatest of these is love.

— Anonymous (Adaptation of 1 Corinthians: 13)

To the Administrator

Suggestions for Using This Book

At a time when Catholic identity is often misunderstood or perceived as peripheral to the academics in Catholic schools, this book has been an attempt to extract the essential elements of Catholic identity as put forth in the Church documents on education to suggest clarification on this vital topic. The following suggestions may assist you in implementing this book with your faculty.

• Design a series of five faculty inservices, each based on a theme of this book (Teacher as Community Builder, Teacher as Committed to Lifelong Spiritual Growth, Teacher as Committed to Lifelong Professional Development, Teacher as Committed to Students' Spiritual Formation, and Teacher as Committed to Students' Human Development). Integrate pertinent "Questions for Reflection" for teachers' private reflection and journalling, and then conduct group-faculty discussions on relevant topics.

• At periodic faculty meetings, invite teachers to reflect on a "Teacher Self-Inventory" (preceding each theme section) and to fill it in privately. After reflection on the inventory, initiate a follow-up discussion involving the faculty's acknowledgment of their overall strengths in the specific theme and areas in which they could improve. Areas that surface could constitute goals and objectives for the upcoming year. After filling in all the inventories, ask faculty to privately assess themselves and to consider dimensions of personal improvement.

• Select a "Question for Reflection" (following each section), and use it as an opening exercise for a faculty meeting.

• Integrate a faculty meeting with an activity suggested in the following section entitled "Additional Faculty Activities." Update your school's philosophy statement by conducting the following with your faculty: "Develop a Mission Statement for Teaching in a Catholic School" and "Formulate a Strategic Vision for Teaching in a Catholic School." Use the activity in the Theme Two section entitled "A Letter to Myself About My Spiritual Journey" to stimulate faculty spiritual reflection. Simply, distribute copies of the handout and instruct participants to reflectively fill in the blanks. Allow approximately 30 minutes for its completion. Then, ask teachers to selectively share parts of their letter with partners. Reconvene with the whole group to encourage voluntary sharing of parts of letters. This type of sharing nurtures the faith-community dimension of a group of faculty.

     • On a routine basis, extract a quote on Catholic identity from the book's chapters and include it in your memoranda to faculty. Do the same with parent newsletters. Integrate quotations in your faculty meetings, retreats, and parent meetings.

     Many areas of the country have been experiencing a teacher exodus from public education to Catholic education. This becomes problematic with subject-matter-qualified applicants who have little understanding of, or interest in, Catholic pedagogy. This book may assist you in delineating those qualities characteristic of promising Catholic school teacher applicants and in formulating interview questions that will adequately assess each applicant's suitability for Catholic education. To further support this end, the following list consists of descriptors derived from the Church documents on education that provide a handy and somewhat detailed portrait of the ideal Catholic educator.

Descriptors of the Ideal Catholic School Educator
(Derived from Church Documents on Education)

1.   **The ideal Catholic school teacher, a community builder—**
   - Contributes to a school atmosphere of respect and cordiality
   - Forms "persons-in-community"
   - Participates in the school's shared vision
   - Respects the tradition of the Catholic Church
   - Affirms the dignity of each student
   - Nurtures student diversity
   - Cultivates a global consciousness
   - Is socially and ecologically aware, locally, nationally, internationally
   - Teaches to peace and justice issues
   - Establishes rapport with students
   - Develops caring student relationships
   - Exercises prudence in student relationships
   - Values dialogue with students
   - Is an active listener
   - Is psychologically present to students
   - Possesses patience and humility
   - Collaborates with colleagues
   - Is a *team player*
   - Builds "authentic" relationships with colleagues
   - Collaborates with parents
   - Creates parent partnerships based on faith
   - Acknowledges parents as primary educators
   - Assists the education of parents
   - Integrates service into the curriculum
   - Creates community outreach opportunities for students
   - Belongs to Catholic and secular professional educational organizations
   - Creates outreach opportunities with other schools, Catholic as well as other private and public schools

2.   **The ideal Catholic school teacher, committed to lifelong spiritual growth—**
- Views himself or herself as a *minister*
- Possesses a *vocation* to Catholic education
- Possesses special qualities of mind and heart
- Models a moral lifestyle and character
- Models Christ's message
- Possesses a love for, and understanding of, today's youth
- Appreciates the *real problems and difficulties* of people
- Is committed to the progress of the apostolate of Catholic education
- Is able to put Christian ideals into practice
- Daily witnesses Christian values to students
- Is committed to student formation
- Is faith-filled
- Understands the concept of integral student formation
- Incorporates pedagogy that emphasizes direct and personal contact with students
- Inspires the educational community with his or her spirituality
- Views his or her role in the Catholic school as an *apostolic mission*
- Understands Catholic doctrine
- Possesses background in theology, ethics, and philosophy
- Is aware of the social teachings of the Church
- Celebrates Christian values through the sacraments
- Displays harmonious interpersonal relationships
- Consistently puts forth effort to be available to students
- Understands that professional competence in the Catholic school includes the commitment to ongoing personal spiritual formation
- Engages in periodic self-evaluation on the authenticity of his or her vocation to Catholic education

3.   **The ideal Catholic school teacher, committed to lifelong professional development—**
- Maintains awareness of the latest advances in teaching methodologies, in psychology, and in the world at large
- Is passionate to improve and expand his or her teaching methods
- Is continually ready to renew and adapt the curriculum
- Is an innovator
- Collaborates with the secular educational community
- Understands that constant and accelerated change characterizes our age and affects every aspect of life
- Envisions new forms of schooling that may more appropriately meet the needs of students
- Experiments in judicious ways to improve educational effectiveness
- Engages in cooperative teaching opportunities with colleagues

4.   **The ideal Catholic school teacher, committed to students' spiritual formation—**
- Provides students with opportunities for worship
- Integrates the Gospel faith dimension throughout the curriculum
- Stimulates students to discover truth and values
- Is committed to forming the minds and hearts of students and guiding them to develop a total commitment to Christ
- Views the act of teaching as holy

- Encourages student self-reflection
- Nurtures students' freedom of inquiry with respect for others
- Fosters conscientious responsibility in students
- Nurtures in students a spirit of solidarity with, and service toward, all other persons
- Cultivates student sensitivity for justice
- Encourages students to become positive agents of change in society
- Employs discovery-based and experiential teaching methodologies in the teaching of religion
- Emphasizes a personalized and participative approach to the religion curriculum
- Recognizes the help of grace in the integral formation of each student
- Instills a sense of Christian service in students

5.   The ideal Catholic school teacher, committed to students' human development—
- Teaches to the whole child
- Personalizes the learning experiences of students
- Meets the unique needs and capabilities of individual students
- Sets high academic standards
- Perceives his or her task as extending beyond the mere transmission of knowledge
- Is committed to the integral education of each student
- Prepares students to become lifelong learners
- Prepares students in the ethical use of technology

Additional Faculty Activities

DREAM LIST

The tenor of the country is one of powerlessness and frustration. Victimization is regularly featured on the typical afternoon TV talk show. Many of our youth do not have a sense of optimism about the future. One concrete way to encourage a sense of hopefulness in students is to use the following activity involving the creation of a dream list. In order to appreciate the effectiveness of this activity with students, teachers may find it beneficial to first do this activity among themselves, perhaps as part of a faculty retreat day.

Leader: Ask the teachers to jot down everything they would like to do for the rest of their lives (can include such mundane items as "to fix a leaky faucet at home" to more lofty goals such as "to pursue a higher degree"). Urge them to come up with as many "dreams" as possible (25, 50, 100!). Then ask them to share with a partner their list of dreams *in the past tense;* for example, "I *completed* my master's degree"; "I *raised* moral, well-adjusted children." After everyone has shared their dreams, ask a couple of volunteers to share their dreams, again in the past tense, with the whole group. Finally, conduct a discussion based upon the following: "What was the effect of this activity? of sharing our dreams in the past tense?" The predictable response is that the activity helps to make future aspirations seem more concrete, thereby instilling in participants the realistic possibility of their accomplishment.

This activity was adapted from one offered by Gail Dusa, a high school teacher who gave a keynote address at the 1992 Self-Esteem Conference, San Jose, CA.

MISSION STATEMENT FOR TEACHING IN A CATHOLIC SCHOOL

Intrinsic to teacher professionalism is the educator's reflection and formulation of his or her philosophy of teaching, an awareness of the philosophical basis for teaching. Whether it is realized or not, teachers' philosophies drive their curricula and instruction, as well as their interaction with students and colleagues. A valuable first step in this process is to ask teachers to formulate a *mission statement*. Sharing one's mission with colleagues and discovering similarities and differences can bring about a shared mission in a school. The following activity facilitates this process.

Leader: Relate the following to the teachers—

Imagine that you have already devoted your life to Catholic education and have recently retired. Take a few moments to look back on your life, the students whose lives you have affected, and ways that you have made a difference. Consider: How would you like to be remembered?

Now, continue and imagine receiving a letter from one of your students. What would you wish to read from this student? How would you like to be remembered? What lasting impression would you wish to have made on this student's life? Jot down your ideas. Discover what these ideas reflect about your true purposes for being in Catholic education. Now, use these ideas to compose your mission statement: several sentences that describe what you are seeking to accomplish most in Catholic education, including the major contributions you wish to make to your students.

As a faculty, share and discuss these statements, and finally, consolidate them into a faculty mission statement.

This activity was adapted from *101 Ways to Develop Student Self-Esteem and Responsibility*, Volumes I and II, by Jack Canfield and Frank Siccone, Allyn & Bacon, 1993.

STRATEGIC VISION FOR TEACHING IN A CATHOLIC SCHOOL

This follow-up activity assists Catholic educators to formulate their philosophical, visionary positions in regard to their teaching. It is a companion to the previous activity.

Leader: Relate the following to teachers—

Ask yourself: What is the greatest achievement that you could imagine accomplishing in your teaching? If Jesus Christ were asking the same question, what would he define as the greatest possible achievement? If you had a student in your class on whom the future of the world depended, what type of educational environment would you wish to provide for that child? What does your choice of environment say about your vision for all students? What do you think is really needed in a Catholic school? What is most needed, from the students' perspectives? from the parents' perspectives? from society's perspective? from the Church's perspective? Now, construct your strategic vision statement, one or two sentences synthesizing your ideas.

As a faculty, share and discuss these statements, and finally, consolidate them into a faculty strategic vision statement.

This activity was adapted from *101 Ways to Develop Student Self-Esteem and Responsibility*, Volumes I and II, by Jack Canfield and Frank Siccone, Allyn & Bacon, 1993.

REFLECTION ON PERSONAL SUCCESSES

The following is an activity designed to build community among adults. It has been adapted from a version entitled "My Strengths" (source unknown) and enables teachers to recognize and appreciate their own gifts as well as the gifts of other teachers. This group activity may provide excellent closure to a staff retreat or may energize staff unity at the opening of the school year.

Materials Needed: Avery stickers (approximately 1³/₄-inch size), pens, and the "Reflection on Personal Successes Worksheet" and "My Strengths" target sheet.

Directions:

1. Distribute the "Reflection on Personal Successes Worksheet" (p. 77) to participants, and ask them to list their most successful life experiences. Allow 20-30 minutes for this reflective period.

2. Then, give each participant a target sheet entitled "My Strengths" (p. 78) and several sheets of Avery stickers. You may wish to group teachers in clusters of five or six according to levels (elementary) or departments (secondary). If the number of faculty is small and if time permits, you may wish to involve everyone in the experience.

3. Instruct participants in the following: Focus on one member of the group at a time. That member is to share (selectively) his or her successful life experiences for a maximum of five minutes. While that member is relating his or her story, the others write on the stickers the qualities they perceive that person to possess. When the member has finished relating his or her experiences, that member then passes the "My Strengths" target sheet to each group member, who, in turn, places all of the stickers on the target and, at the same time, articulates to the individual the qualities perceived. This process is repeated until each group member's target has been filled.

4. When everyone has completed the activity, reconvene to reflect upon the following questions:
   - What value did this experience have for you?
   - Did you encounter any difficulties? revelations?
   - What implications does this activity have for us as a faculty?
   - How can we continue to build upon what we began today throughout the school year?
   - What implications does this type of activity have for our students?

Reflection on Personal Successes Worksheet

List one or more of your *successful experiences* at specific stages of your life. Include experiences that involve the following areas of self-growth: physical, emotional, intellectual, and spiritual. Many of us consider our successes *externally*; consider *internal* successes, as well. (Continue on the back of this sheet if needed.)

Early Childhood Years—

Elementary School Years—

High School Years—

College Years—

Teaching Career—

From Your Family—

Other—

• Have you had any successes that have benefitted others? Explain.

• My definition of success is:

My Strengths

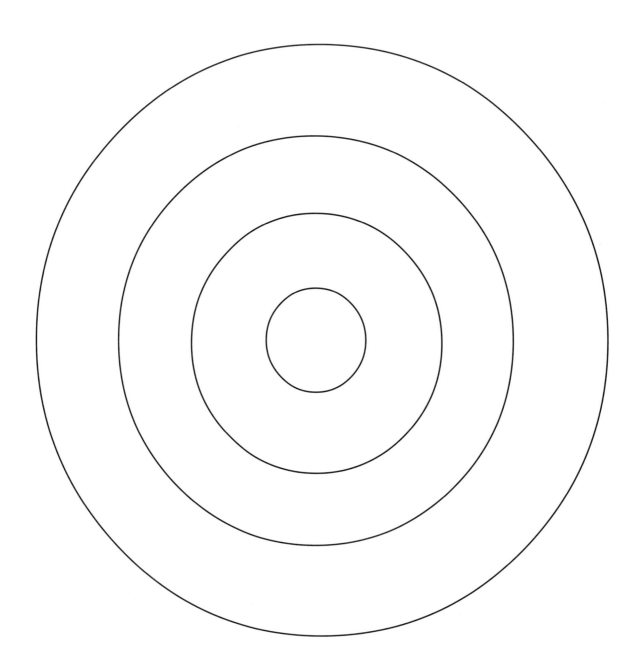

Appendixes

Appendix A

Percentage of Text in Church Documents on Education* Devoted to Themes Descriptive of the Ideal Catholic School Teacher

Teacher as Community Builder	27.0%
Teacher as Committed to Lifelong Spiritual Growth	25.8%
Teacher as Committed to Lifelong Professional Development	3.3%
Teacher as Committed to Students' Spiritual Formation	40.0%
Teacher as Committed to Students' Human Development	3.9%

*Documents Analyzed (Shimabukuro, 1993):
> *Declaration on Christian Education* (1965)
> *To Teach as Jesus Did* (1972)
> *Teach Them* (1976)
> *The Catholic School* (1977)
> *Sharing the Light of Faith: National Catechetical Directory for Catholics of the United States* (1979)
> *Lay Catholics in Schools: Witnesses to Faith* (1982)
> *The Religious Dimension of Education in a Catholic School* (1988)
> *In Support of Catholic Elementary and Secondary Schools* (1990)

Appendix B

Subthemes Descriptive of the Ideal Catholic School Teacher Extracted from Church Documents on Education[*]

Teacher as Community Builder:
> Recognizes the dignity of each student
> Appreciates student diversity (talents, culture, religion)
>   and instills this appreciation in students
> Builds Christian community in the school
> Builds relationships with students
> Forms "persons-in-community"
> Educates to peace and justice
> Collaborates with colleagues
> Collaborates with parents
> Participates in the shared Christian vision of the
>   school community
> Collaborates with the human community outside the school

Teacher as Committed to Lifelong Spiritual Growth:
> Realizes the importance of Catholic education to the
>   Church and greater society
> Regards the teaching profession as a vocation
> Models Christian values
> Undergoes spiritual/religious formation
> Routinely engages in self-evaluation on the authenticity
>   of his or her vocation to Catholic education

Teacher as Committed to Lifelong Professional Development:
> Is carefully prepared in secular pedagogy
> Remains updated in psychology, pedagogy, and the
>   intellectual sciences

Teacher as Committed to Students' Spiritual Formation:
> Integrates the Christian message—community, worship,
>   and service—into his or her teaching
> Integrates religious truth and values with life
>   (culture) throughout the curriculum
> Promotes the spiritual/religious formation and
>   transformation of students
> Instills a sense of Christian service in students

Teacher as Committed to Students' Human Development:
> Prepares students to be lifelong learners
> Personalizes the learning experiences of students
> Equips students with high academic standards
> Prepares students for professional life
> Develops intellectual faculties of students
> Educates the whole child

Prepares students in the ethical use of technology
Instructs students in social skills
Instructs students in human sexuality

*Documents Analyzed (Shimabukuro, 1993):
Declaration on Christian Education (1965)
To Teach as Jesus Did (1972)
Teach Them (1976)
The Catholic School (1977)
Sharing the Light of Faith: National Catechetical Directory for Catholics of the United States (1979)
Lay Catholics in Schools: Witnesses to Faith (1982)
The Religious Dimension of Education in a Catholic School (1988)
In Support of Catholic Elementary and Secondary Schools (1990)

References and
Additional Resources

Bowman, L. E. (1990). *Teaching for Christian hearts, souls and minds.* San Francisco: Harper & Row.

Buetow, H. A. (1988). *The Catholic school: Its roots, identity, and future.* New York: Crossroad.

Bryk, A. S., & Holland, P. (1984). Research provides perspectives on effective Catholic schools. *Momentum, 15,* 12-16.

Bryk, A. S., Lee, V., & Holland, P. (1993). *Catholic schools and the common good.* Cambridge, MA: Harvard University Press.

Ciriello, M. (1987). *Teachers in Catholic schools: A study of commitment.* Unpublished doctoral dissertation, Catholic University of America.

Congregation for Catholic Education. (1988). *The religious dimension of education in a Catholic school.* Boston: Daughters of St. Paul.

Convey, J. (1992). *Catholic schools make a difference: Twenty-five years of research.* Washington, DC: National Catholic Educational Association.

Costello, G. (April/May, 1991). Meeting Jesus face to face. *Religion Teacher's Journal.*

Cummings, J. (1996). *The impact of non-Catholic students on the perceived Catholic identity of Catholic secondary schools.* Unpublished doctoral dissertation, University of San Francisco.

Daues, M. A. (1983). *The modern Catholic teacher: A role analysis in the post-Vatican II schools.* Unpublished doctoral dissertation, Fordham University.

Dorsey, J. (1992). *The role of the Catholic elementary teacher as model of Gospel values.* Unpublished doctoral dissertation, University of San Francisco.

Gardner, H. (1983). *Frames of mind: The theory of multiple intelligences.* New York: Basic Books.

Groome, T. (1996). What makes a school Catholic? In J. O'Keefe (Ed.), *The contemporary Catholic school: Context, identity and diversity.* Great Britain: Biddles Ltd., Guildford and King's Lynn.

Harris, M. (1987). *Teaching and religious imagination.* San Francisco: Harper & Row.

Hastings, A. (Ed.). (1991). Catholic history from Vatican I to John Paul II. *Modern Catholicism: Vatican II and after.* New York: Oxford University Press.

Helbling, M., & Kushner, R. (1995). *The people who work there: The report of the Catholic elementary school teacher survey.* Washington, DC: National Catholic Educational Association.

Martin, J. R. (1992). *The schoolhome: Rethinking schools for changing families.* Cambridge, MA: Harvard University Press.

McBrien, R. P. (1980). *Catholicism* (Vol. 2). San Francisco: Harper & Row.

McDade, J. (1991). Catholic theology in the post-conciliar period. In A. Hastings (Ed.), *Modern Catholicism: Vatican II and after.* New York: Oxford University Press.

National Conference of Catholic Bishops. (1972). *To teach as Jesus did.* Washington, DC: United States Catholic Conference.

National Conference of Catholic Bishops. (1976). *Teach them.* Washington, DC: United States Catholic Conference.

National Conference of Catholic Bishops. (1979). *Sharing the light of faith: National catechetical directory for Catholics of the United States.* Washington, DC: United States Catholic Conference.

National Conference of Catholic Bishops. (1990). *In support of Catholic elementary and secondary schools.* Washington, DC: United States Catholic Conference.

Nouwen, H. (1971). *Creative ministry.* New York: Doubleday.

Nuzzi, R. (1996). *Gifts of the spirit: Multiple intelligences in religious education.* Washington, DC: National Catholic Educational Association.

Palmer, P. (1985). *To know as we are known: A spirituality of education.* San Francisco: Harper & Row.

Palmer, P. (1998). *The courage to teach: Exploring the inner landscape of a teacher's life.* San Francisco: Jossey-Bass.

Peck, M. S. (1987). *The different drum: Community making and peace.* New York: Simon & Schuster.

Rahner, K. (1968). *Spirit in the world.* New York: Herder and Herder.

Rahner, K. (1972). The Second Vatican Council's challenge to theology. *Theological investigations IX.* London: Darton, Longman and Todd.

Reck, C. (1991). *The Catholic identity of Catholic schools.* Washington, DC: National Catholic Educational Association.

Sacred Congregation for Catholic Education. (1977). *The Catholic school.* Washington, DC: United States Catholic Conference.

Sacred Congregation for Catholic Education. (1982). *Lay Catholics in schools: Witnesses to faith.* Boston: Daughters of St. Paul.

Schön, D. (1983). *The reflective practitioner.* New York: Basic Books.

Schultz, T., & Schultz, J. (1993). *Why nobody learns much of anything at church: And how to fix it.* Loveland, CO: Group Publishing.

Second Vatican Council. (1988). Declaration on Christian education. In A. Flannery (Ed.), *Vatican Council II: The conciliar and post conciliary documents* (Vol. 1, rev. ed.). Northport, NY: Costello Publishing. (Original work published 1965)

Secondary Schools Department. (1987). *The Catholic high school teacher: Building on research.* Washington, DC: National Catholic Educational Association.

Shimabukuro, G. (1994). In search of identity. *Momentum, 15,* 23-26.

Shimabukuro, V. (1993). *Profile of an ideal Catholic school teacher: Content analysis of Roman and American documents, 1965 to 1990.* Unpublished doctoral dissertation, University of San Francisco.

About the Author

Gini Shimabukuro, Ed.D., began her teaching career at the Catholic elementary level. She is currently an assistant professor and the associate director of the Institute for Catholic Educational Leadership at the University of San Francisco. When engaged in her doctoral studies, she became intrigued with the issue of Catholic identity as expressed through teachers. This book is the result of her research. She is very interested in curriculum, instructional design and its delivery in Catholic schools, as well as Catholic school identity and the preparation of Catholic school personnel. She delights in time spent with her husband and two college-age sons.